Su-57 Felon

PIOTR BUTOWSKI

KEY
Books

MODERN MILITARY AIRCRAFT SERIES, VOLUME 2

Front cover image: The newest Sukhoi Su-57 Felon fighter is now entering service and will be the essential combat aircraft in Russia for the next few decades. (Vadim Savitsky/Russia's MoD)

Back cover image: A Sukhoi Su-57 is accompanied by the smaller MiG-35 multirole fighter produced by the RSK MiG company. (Piotr Butowski)

Title page image: A pair of Su-57s, T-50-2 (left) and T-50-5R, demonstrates sharp manoeuvrings during the MAKS 2019 airshow. (Piotr Butowski)

Contents page image: The fifth-generation Su-57 features stealth configuration, supersonic speed and manoeuvrability, and the latest sensors and weaponry. (Piotr Butowski)

Published by Key Books
An imprint of Key Publishing Ltd
PO Box 100
Stamford
Lincs
PE19 1XQ

www.keypublishing.com

The right of Piotr Butowski to be identified as the author of this book has been asserted in accordance with the Copyright, Designs and Patents Act 1988 Sections 77 and 78.

Copyright © Piotr Butowski, 2021

ISBN 978 1 913870 44 7

Typeset by SJmagic DESIGN SERVICES, India.

Contents

Introduction

In December 2020, the first new-generation Su-57 Felon fighter was formally handed over to the Russian Aerospace Forces (VKS – Vozdushno-Kosmicheskiye Sily). On 24 December 2020, the Su-57 '01' took off from airfield of the Sukhoi Komsomolsk-on-Amur Aviation Plant (KnAAZ) and headed west. After two stops, one in Ulan-Ude and the other in Novosibirsk, the aircraft arrived in Akhtubinsk, the site of the Ministry of Defence's 929th State Flight Test Centre.

Thus, after 11 years of testing, the implementation of the Su-57 into service began. In 2021, the VKS is to receive four more fighters, and by 2028, three 24-ship regiments are to be armed with Su-57s.

Russia's path towards developing a fifth-generation fighter has been a long one. The Soviet Union began to develop a new air superiority fighter at approximately the same time as the United States launched its Advanced Tactical Fighter programme.

The first Su-57 '01' was delivered to the Russia's Ministry of Defence in December 2020. The fighter is operated by the 929th Flight Test Centre at Akhtubinsk. (KnAAZ)

Chapter 1

The First Approach: MiG MFI

onceptual work on the next-generation fighters began in 1983 with the introduction of the fourth-generation MiG-29 Fulcrum and Su-27 Flanker fighters into serial production and service. The Air Force formulated the first general requirements in the scientific research work codenamed 'Palma' (palm), and then in the I-90 (Istrebitel, (fighter for the nineties)) programme. On 19 June 1986, these intentions were confirmed by a government resolution launching two projects: heavy fighter MFI (Mnogofunktsyonalnyi Frontovoi Istrebitel, also designated izdeliye 1.42 or izdeliye 5.12) and lightweight LFI (L for Lyogkiy, izdeliye 4.12), using common aerodynamic schemes. Both aircraft were built at the Mikoyan design bureau (OKB MiG); Sukhoi was then tasked with developing a T-60S medium bomber to replace the Tu-22M Backfire, as well as an experimental S-22 fighter with a forward-swept wing, which, however, was given a much lower priority than the MFI/LFI. According to the 1986 schedule, the heavy MFI and its downscaled simple version LFI were to enter service in 2001 and replace the Su-27 and MiG-29 pair. In 1988, the LFI project was frozen and put back five years to 2006; the MFI was considered to be the carrier of new technologies, and the LFI could arise later as the simplified lightweight variant.

The most important feature of the MFI fighter is already in its name: multi-functional. The aircraft was to combine the capabilities of an air superiority fighter and an interceptor, as well as a strike and reconnaissance aircraft; versions of the 1.42P interceptor, 1.42R reconnaissance aircraft and the 1.42K ship-borne fighter for the next Soviet aircraft carriers under construction were planned. The chief designer (the head of the project) of the MiG MFI was Grigory Sedov; in the past he was a test pilot and the chief designer of the MiG-23 and MiG-27 Flogger aircraft. General supervision of the project was performed by the OKB MiG designer General Rostislav Belyakov. After Sedov's retirement in 1997, Yuri Vorotnikov took charge of the MFI programme.

Left: Designer General Rostislav Belyakov provided supervision of the project of the first Soviet fifth-generation fighter MiG MFI. (Piotr Butowski)

Right: Grigory Sedov, former test pilot, was the head of the MiG MFI project between 1986 and 1997. (Piotr Butowski)

Yevgeny Fedosov, head of the GosNIIAS institute dealing with aviation systems, said at a press conference in January 1999 that the MFI was subject to 'three S' requirements. The first S was 'sverkhzvuk': supersonic cruising speed and – more importantly – the ability to conduct air combat at supersonic speed. This places particular demands on the engines (high thrust without afterburning), on the aerodynamic configuration (the capability of achieving high g-loads in supersonic flight, rather than subsonic in previous aircraft) and on the weapon systems (short response times). The reason why a supersonic cruising speed was requested was the need to shorten the aircraft's response time to a call. In addition, a long range in supersonic flight was required, which is justified by the geographic size of Russia and the sparse airfield network, especially in the north.

The second S was extreme manoeuvrability, i.e. it can achieve angles of attack of 60–70° while maintaining controllability and even has the ability to reach angles of attack of 100° for a short time without losing stability, though at this angle it cannot manoeuvre. This places great demands on the aircraft's aerodynamic configuration and its control system. The standard solution becomes the engine's thrust vectoring. Super manoeuvrability is needed by an aircraft to attack targets in any position, including from the rear, in close air combat. For the same purpose, the aircraft's weapons system was to include a small rear-looking radar, highly manoeuvrable air-to-air missiles with gas-dynamic control and a movable 30mm cannon. The primary type of heavy fighter operation is long- and medium-range combat, but the transition to close air combat is also likely, Fedosov said.

The third S was the requirement for reduced visibility (stealth). However, the 'stealth' technology was to be implemented only when it did not violate the first two S requirements. In particular, this means that changes to the shape of the aircraft due to 'stealth' requirements should be small, as any such change is detrimental to speed or manoeuvrability.

Other requirements of the Soviet Air Force presented to the MFI included the automation of the aircraft's fire-control and self-defence systems, a high level of autonomy of operation, thanks to the exchange of information with other aircraft and ground stations and the tactical situation screen in the cockpit, as well as short take-off and landing.

According to the results of research conducted at the Central Aerohydrodynamic Institute (TsAGI), the canard configuration was selected for the MiG 1.42 to ensure high manoeuvrability at supersonic speed. The shoulder-mounted, delta-shaped wing with moderate sweepback had no anhedral or dihedral angle.

Large-area swept all-moving canard foreplanes, fitted above the wing plane, acted as control surfaces and also increased lift at high angles of attack (that is, fulfilled the role of wing leading-edge root extensions in fourth-generation aircraft). A 'dogtooth' at the leading-edge generated vortex. The fairings to support canards were exceptionally large, to cover large-pitch and high-power actuators. Two-section large-area elevons at the trailing edge and two-segment leading-edge flaps were fitted. Twin widely spaced outward-canted (approx. 15°) tailfins and inset rudders were carried on short wing-trailing edge booms. Twin ventral fins with movable rear sections were fitted to the same booms. Additional rear flaps installed between engines and tail booms acted as elevators and increased the allowable range of change of the centre-of-gravity position.

All these surfaces, as well as the deflection of the moving engines nozzles, were controlled by the digital fly-by-wire KSU-1.42 (Kompleksnaya Sistema Upravleniya) flight control system developed by the Moscow company Avionika. According to the company, 'the wing, fuselage, empennage and movable thrust vector, combined with the comprehensive KSU flight control system, create a uniform aerodynamic surface that adapts to all flight ranges'. The fighter's static instability was claimed to be very high, probably much more than 10%. Thanks to the ample high-lift devices and vectored thrust, the aircraft can also operate from short runways. MiG MFI had no air brakes; that role was played by differential tilting rudders and ventral fins.

A large part of the aerodynamics tests of the new fighter, especially unstable flight ranges, were carried out on the air-dropped model DM5.12, made by the design facility of the Kharkiv Aviation Institute (KhAI). The DM5.12 model, made on a scale of 1:4.5, had a weight of 480–520kg, depending on the configuration tested; after it was dropped from under a Mi-8 helicopter or Tu-16LL bomber, it flew for 2.5 minutes at an altitude of up to 7,000m, reaching speeds of up to 150m/s and landed on a parachute. 128 flight parameters were recorded. Two DM5.12 models were tested from 1987 to 1992; in total they made ten flights.

The single pilot had a new ejection seat described as a 'variable-geometry seat' by test pilot Anatoly Kvochur. It automatically adjusted in flight depending on the g-load, to almost a horizontal position. Also, the pilot's suit was to be quite new. The pilot cockpit of 1.42 was common for MiG aircraft with a deeply positioned seat and limited visibility to the rear.

In the 1.42's shape, you didn't see much fascination with the 'stealth' idea. The reduction of the radar cross-section was achieved by using composites in the airframe construction and painting it with radiation-absorbing paint. Composites account for about 30% of the structure; in particular, the air intakes are completely composite. The engine air ducts are S curved to shield the engine compressors, one of the most visible structural features on the radar. On the 1.44 prototype, there is no internal weapons compartment, but there is a recess under the fuselage, suggesting a conformal missile container; the internal weapons compartment was planned for the 1.42. During the presentation of the aircraft in 1999, the then MiG designer General Mikhail Korzhuyev said that 'in reducing visibility we achieved characteristics not worse than the F-22'.

New generation engines were ordered for the new generation aircraft. Unusually for MiG aircraft, the engines, which were most often made by the Soyuz company, were this time ordered from the rival Lyulka team, led at the time by Viktor Chepkin. The MFI was powered by two low-bypass ratio AL-41F (izdeliye 20) turbofan engines. They achieved a maximum thrust with afterburning of about 39,342lbf (175kN). The AL-41F engine had a unit thrust (thrust to dry-weight ratio) of approximately 10:1 compared to 8:1 for the AL-31F engine of Su-27. The AL-41F had axis-symmetrical movable 3-D nozzles (probably +/-15° vertically and +/-8° horizontally).

The AL-41F engine had passed a fairly large range of tests, including in the air. In 1993, tests began on the Tu-16LL (Letayushchaya Laboratoriya) flying testbed, and later on the experimental LL-84-20 aircraft, which was the MiG-25P (izdeliye 84) with one standard R-15BD-300 engine and one AL-41F (izdeliye 20) in the left nacelle. The LL-84-20 performed 22 test flights, including those at speeds of

The MiG 1.44 is powered by two Lyulka AL-41F (izdeliye 20) turbofans with movable nozzles. Several control surfaces are seen alongside, including a flap between the engine and tail boom, and a movable rear section of the ventral fin. (Piotr Butowski)

more than 1,080kts (2,000km/h) and altitudes of over 65,620ft (20,000m). In total, 27 AL-41F engines were produced in the Lyulka-Saturn test workshops. In September 1998, an agreement was signed to start serial production of AL-41F at the Rybinsk engine plant, but it was never implemented.

The main task of the MFI was to gain air superiority in combat at long and medium distances, guiding missiles to several distanced air targets simultaneously. In close air combat, the fighter was to engage targets in any position, including at the rear. Consequently, the MFI was to receive the Phazotron-NIIR Sh109 radar system enabling all-round coverage that included triple-antenna N014 electronically scanned phased array radar in the nose, as well as rearward-facing N015 radar in the tail. A highly automated fire-control system was to join, apart from radar, and was linked to the electro-optical sight and a helmet-mounted sight and display. Also, navigation, communications/data exchange and electronic warfare systems were to be integrated with the fire-control system.

The new generation of air-to-air weapons designed for the MFI included the long-range K-37M, medium-range K-77M and close air combat K-30 missiles; the typical load for air combat consisted of four K-77M and four K-30 missiles. The aircraft's radar was also to enable operations against ground targets and the use of all types of Russian air-to-ground tactical guided weapons. According to official statements, the aircraft was supposed to receive a 30mm cannon, but it was absent on the 1.44 prototype.

The Ups and Downs of the MFI project

For several successive years everything had been running to schedule. In 1991, the MFI preliminary design and the aircraft mock-up were approved by a state committee, and construction of the first proof-of-concept demonstrator without mission systems, designated izdeliye 1.44, went on in the MiG design bureau workshop at Moscow in co-operation with the Sokol plant in Nizhny Novgorod (then Gorky). It did not yet have the target equipment, including radar, and was intended only for testing the aerodynamics, engines and the control system. It was planned to build five test aircraft, gradually growing in functions.

In 1994, the aircraft was almost complete and on July 14, it was carried to Zhukovsky for flight tests. 'Almost' turned out to be a decisive word. Before an aircraft is allowed to perform its maiden flight, a specific range of tests of its components is required. In particular, the engine should be tested to ensure its operation within 30–50 hours. Meanwhile, due to a lack of resources, the AL-41F engine underwent tests that guaranteed only 5–15 hours of operation. The aircraft was still devoid of final actuators for the control system. The 1.44 had a very high degree of static instability and to keep it in the air, continuous operation of a very powerful control system was necessary. For this reason, the first attempt of aircraft take-off, made by pilot Roman Taskayev on 15 December 1994, was a failure. There was no more money, and the aircraft had to spend several years in a hangar, waiting for better times.

A big blow to the MFI programme was the organisational changes at the MiG company or, more precisely, the incorporation of the design bureau into the MAPO production plant, which took place in May 1995. The design facility lost its financial independence, and the MAPO plant was not interested in continuing experimental work on an aircraft with little chance of being ordered by the Russian Air Force or being exported. There was a policy of doing only what the Defence Ministry would pay for – and it paid nothing.

It was only possible to bring the aircraft to flight tests after the company's management changed its attitude towards it. In September 1997, with the arrival of Mikhail Korzhuyev as the MiG design bureau general manager and general designer, flying 1.44 became one of the company's priorities. In the same month, Sukhoi flew his prototype of the S-37 (Su-47) fighter, competing for MFI. Thus, raising the 1.44 in the air became a matter of 'company honour'. Mikhail Korzhuyev convinced the most important sub-suppliers of this idea, and they agreed to prepare the AL-41F engines and the control system for tests at their own expense.

On 12 January 1999, the only presentation for many years of the 1.44 took place at Zhukovsky. The 1.44 demonstrator was intended only for testing a new aerodynamic shape; it had no mission systems and weapons yet. (Piotr Butowski)

On 12 January 1999, several hundred guests were invited to the aircraft industry's test airfield in Zhukovsky near Moscow, including foreign military attachés, journalists and me. Russian Defence Minister Igor Sergeyev and the Air Force Commander-in-Chief Anatoly Kornukov arrived. The exhibition of MiG production was waiting for the guests: a modernised MiG-21-98 fighter; a model of the MiG-23-98 modernisation; two versions of the MiG-AT trainer, the export 821 and the Russian 823; modernised MiG-29SMT and MiG-29UBT fighters; a ship-borne MiG-29K fighter; and, finally, a modernised MiG-31BM interceptor. However, these people weren't gathering for them: the main actor of this presentation was the 1.44 aircraft, the first prototype of the MiG MFI fighter – the most secret of Russian aircraft. The existence of the MFI had been known about for several years, but none of the bystanders had seen it. At 11:00 exactly, a strange silhouette appeared far away on the taxiway. The aircraft taxied over to the crowd and the pilot, Vladimir Gorbunov, got out of the cockpit. This is how the world saw the 1.44 aircraft for the first time. In the Air Standards Co-ordinating Committee, the MiG MFI received the code name 'Flatpack'.

The aircraft taxied the guests invited to the presentation, but it was still not ready for flight. Nevertheless, a year later, at its own risk, MiG management decided to start flight tests. On 29 February 2000, at 11:25 local time, pilot Vladimir Gorbunov took off for the first time and made two circles around the airfield in Zhukovsky; two weeks earlier, on 16 February, the aircraft had made a high-speed taxi run. The flight lasted 18 minutes and proceeded at an altitude of 1,000m with a speed of 500–600km/h. According to the pilot, 'the airplane obeyed, but it was obvious that in terms of flight handling, it is a principally new machine. We still have a lot of work to do.' The second flight, on 27 April 2000, lasted 22 minutes; the aircraft retracted the landing gear. No further risks were taken and the MiG 1.44 never took off again, remaining in the history of aviation as the most expensive aircraft when counting the cost of one minute in the air.

The MiG company, unfortunately, did not take care of the images of the aircraft in flight; both flights were only filmed in poor quality from a spotter aircraft. After another change in the management of the MiG company, the interest in this aircraft ended, and it stayed in the hangar for many years. In another burst of interest, the aircraft got a new livery with a tricolour Russian ribbon on the tailfins and a large number 144 (previously, it carried the trivial number 01); however, it ended there. In August 2015, at Moscow's International Aviation and Space Salon (MAKS) exhibition, the MiG 1.44 fighter was first shown to the general public; it appeared in the historical section of the exhibition.

MiG MFI (1.42) Design Specifications

Wingspan	17.0m
Length	21.7m
Nominal take-off weight	28,600kg
Maximum take-off weight	34,000kg
Maximum allowable take-off weight	37,000kg
Maximum fuel	13,000kg
Maximum weapons and stores	8,500kg
Maximum speed	Mach 2.35
Supersonic cruising speed	Mach 1.5
Maximum supersonic range	1,850km
Maximum range	4,000km

Left: The heavy MiG MFI fighter was to be the Soviet equivalent of the American ATF (today's F-22A). However, it ended up with one 1.44 technology demonstrator that made just two flights. (Piotr Butowski)

Below: MiG 1.44 returns to its hangar after the presentation on 12 January 1999. (Piotr Butowski)

The MiG 1.44 performed only two flights, on 19 February and 27 April 2000; in the second flight, the aircraft retracted its landing gear. (RSK MiG)

Right and below: The MiG 1.44 was only shown to the general public for the first time in 2015; it appeared in the historical section of the MAKS 2015 exhibition. (Piotr Butowski)

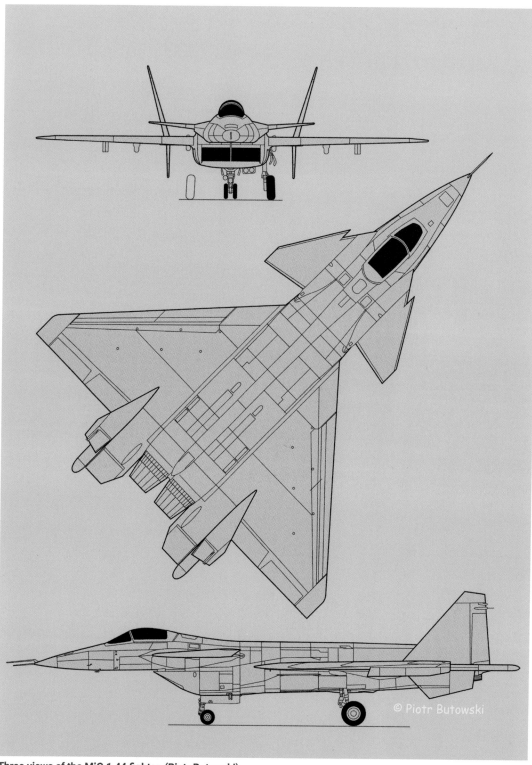

Three views of the MiG 1.44 fighter. (Piotr Butowski)

© Piotr Butowski

Chapter 2

Sukhoi Su-47 with a Forward-Swept Wing

In the same 1983, when Mikoyan started working at MFI, the Sukhoi design bureau secured an order for the S-22 experimental fighter. The status of the work carried out by Sukhoi at the time was much lower than that of the MiG project; the S-22 was an industry research programme that was to end with the construction of an aerodynamic proof-of-concept aircraft.

What made the S-22 fighter stand out was the forward-swept wing. Work on such a wing, which was carried out in the USSR quite intensively right after World War Two, was discontinued in 1952 because of its lack of perspective. Both in wind tunnels and on real aircraft, it has been shown that the strong torsional moments in such a wing cannot be overcome with the existing (metal) technology and cause the wing to deform. However, every idea comes back after some time. The TsAGI institute started to test the forward-swept wings again in 1978, after receiving news of a similar project in the USA (the experimental Grumman X-29A started flight tests in 1984). The return to this configuration was made possible by new composite materials that were then available in aviation. The directional deformation of deflection and torsion was used: with the proper arrangement of the fibres of the composite wing covering, their deformation counteracts the deformation of the wing. In the TsAGI wind tunnels, the behaviour of such a wing was tested in a wide range of speeds from Mach 0.2 to Mach 2.0 and angles of attack of up to 80°. Most of the advantages were found at transonic speeds, between Mach 0.8 and 1.3, which is where the majority of air combat takes place. The forward-swept wing has less drag and a greater lift-to-drag ratio than a normal wing; below this range, both wings are equal, while above this range a usual swept wing has the advantage. At high angles of attack, the lift force of the forward-swept wing is greater than that of the back oblique wing; the effectiveness of ailerons is also greater, while that of tailplanes is less. Together, this means better manoeuvrability, longer range and shorter take-off and landing.

Air-dropped scale models SLM22 and SLM32 made by the Kharkiv Aviation Institute were used for the tests of unstable flight ranges. (KhAI)

Between 1983 and 1988, eight configurations of the S-22 fighter were tested, ranging from a shape very similar to the X-29A and ending with a fighter with a wing with inverse sweep, big wing-root extensions and several effective control planes (canard foreplanes, elevons and control flaps behind the wings), as well as a thrust-vectored engine.

The programme's status goes up

In 1988, after seeing the promising results of the first studies, Sukhoi obtained a change in the status of the project from an experiment to a fully fledged next-generation fighter development programme; with this change, the aircraft received the new designation S-32. Since the aircraft was intended primarily as a successor to the Su-27K (Su-33) ship-borne fighter for Soviet aircraft carriers, it also received the designation Su-27KM. Mikhail Pogosyan, the later head of the Sukhoi concern (and now the rector of Moscow Aviation Institute), became the chief designer of the S-32, under the general supervision of Sukhoi's general designer Mikhail Simonov. Since 1998, the project was headed by Sergey Korotkov, who is the current general designer at the United Aircraft Corporation (UAC). According to the schedule at that time, the S-32 prototype was to start flight tests in 1991–92, and the serial production of the fighter was already planned to be launched at the Irkutsk plant in 1996–97. The Irkutsk plant was also expected to build three S-32 prototypes: one static and two for flight evaluations.

Some of the aerodynamics tests of the new Sukhoi fighter, especially the unstable flight range tests, were carried out on dynamically similar scale models, SLM22 and SLM32, made by the design facility of the KhAI. The first two SLM22 models, corresponding to the first S-22 design, were built in 1987 and made three flights. The SLM22 model was made on a scale of 1:4, had a weight of 900kg and had no engine; it was dropped from the external suspension on a 40m rope under a Mi-8 helicopter. After the drop, the model entered the dive, and after reaching the required speed, it performed the flight programme; it landed on a parachute with additional shock absorbers. In 1995, another SLM32 model corresponding to the S-32 project was launched. Unlike the previous SLM22, it had propulsion and a small M-601M jet engine. The SLM32 model weighed 1,200kg and flew for 10 minutes at an altitude of 5,000m; the equipment recorded 128 flight parameters. The last of the eight SLM32 flights was performed in 1999.

The aerodynamic configuration of the Su-47 is relatively complicated. It is a 'tandem triplane' (canard, wing and tailplane) with large oval wing leading-edge root extensions (LERX) above the

Left: Mikhail Simonov, Sukhoi's Designer General when the Su-47 was developed. (Piotr Butowski)

Right: Sergey Korotkov, the current General Designer of the United Aircraft Corporation (UAC), headed the Su-47 programme in 1990–2000s. (Piotr Butowski)

air intakes, large trapezoidal canards (foreplanes), then a 20° forward-swept wing, and 75° swept tailplanes. The wing is made up of 90% composites. The tailfins are similar to those of the Su-27 but are slightly tilted to the sides (in the Su-27 the fins are parallel to each other). The wing's high-lift devices are typical and consist of ailerons and rear and front flaps. It is operated by the quadruple digital fly-by wire SDU-427 flight control system made by MNPK Avionika of Moscow. The air inlets are fixed, located under the wing LERXes and have a circular section.

In the original 1988 design, the aircraft was to be powered by two Salyut R79M-300 or R179-300 engines with a thrust of approximately 18,500kg, being a development of the R79V-300 engines from the Yak-41 vertical take-off and landing fighter. Later, it was planned to replace them with a new generation Lyulka AL-41F with similar thrust, the same as in the MiG MFI. The engines were to have flat moving nozzles.

The aircraft was to receive the RLPK-32 radar system developed by the Tikhomirov NIIP company of Zhukovsky, with an electronic scanning radar (probably of the N011M type) in front and a small N012 radar looking back. A basic weapon set was to be carried inside two fuselage weapons bays. One of them, about 4.5m long and 2.2m wide, was placed in the central part of fuselage, between the main undercarriage. The other smaller bay (a length of 3.8m, with a width narrowing from 1.4m in the rear to 0.8m in front), located in front of the bigger one, extended to the front wheel. The air-to-air armament was to include long-range K-28, medium-range K-77 and close air combat K-74 air-to-air missiles; in the future, the use of new ultra-long-range K-100 and short-range K-30 missiles was planned.

The programme's status goes down

However, in the early 1990s, there was no money in the USSR for new aircraft. The S-32 programme was increasingly delayed; its status fell back to the level of experimental work and the Ministry of Defence (MoD) ceased funding it. The Sukhoi company invested its own funds from the sale of the Su-27 to China, to complete the S-32. There was not much money, however, and the designers decided to simplify the S-32 prototype. Instead of the new generation engines, the most powerful available Aviadvigatel D-30F11 (izdeliye 70) engines were used; the D-30F11 was a 34,304lbf (152.6kN) thrust modification of the D-30F6 engine from the MiG-31 interceptor. Neither the planned RLPK-32 radar, nor most other equipment and weapons were completed. In the construction of the aircraft, elements from the Su-27 family fighters were used, including the vertical tail and landing gear. The construction of a separate airframe for static tests was abandoned; the same aircraft was first tested in summer

1996 with initial strength tests. Then the assembly was completed and the equipment necessary for flight tests was fitted. In May 1997, the aircraft was taken to Zhukovsky.

Model of S-32 fighter in the planned carrier-based Su-27KM fighter variant with flat engine nozzles. Underneath the fuselage there is – not visible in the picture – a brake hook for landing on an aircraft carrier. (Piotr Butowski)

At the end of 1996, information about the preparations for the first S-32 flight appeared in the Western press. This caused a lot of confusion in Russia and, after appropriate deliberation, it was decided to 'take countermeasures': the designation of the aircraft was changed to S-37. Sukhoi's spokesman, Yuri Chervakov, could safely say that 'there is no S-32 aircraft'. Looking ahead: after starting trials in 1997, the S-37 was named Berkut (golden eagle), and in 2000, the Sukhoi design bureau renamed it again to the Su-47. Within NATO, the Su-47 is codenamed 'Firkin'.

The first flight of the test aircraft, now designated the S-37-1, took place on 25 September 1997 at 15:09 at the airfield in Zhukovsky, with Igor Votintsev at the controls. The new S-37-1 was accompanied on its first 30-minute flight by an Su-30 two-seater recording the event on film. On its fourth flight, on 13 October, the S-37-1 retracted its landing gear for the first time. The trials gradually gained momentum; in 1997, the aircraft flew eight times, in 1998, 23 times, and in December 2000, it made its 100th flight. On 24 January 2000, the aircraft exceeded the speed of sound for the first time, reaching Mach 1.3. In August 1999, Berkut was shown to a wide audience for the first time, initially at the Aviation Day in Tushino and a few days later at the MAKS exhibition in Zhukovsky. Until 2005, the Su-47 appeared in public several times, but only in flight; it has never been directly accessible.

The Su-47 has never been a priority for the Russian Air Force. It is significant that for the official presentation of the fighter in Zhukovsky on 18 October 1997, only the 'third official suit' arrived; it can be noted that the Minister of Defence and the Air Force Commander-in-Chief came to the MiG 1.44 presentation in January 1999. Much earlier, on 31 January and 1 February 1996, a meeting of the Military Council of the Russian Air Force with the heads of the design bureaus was held, during which a fundamental and unfavourable decision for the Su-47 was made: the military assessed that, 'the aircraft is not prospective from the point of view of rearmament of the Air Force in 2010–2025.'

In 2006, another phase of the Su-47 tests began. These were intended to test the internal weapons bay for the future Su-57 (PAK FA); the bay was arranged in the bottom of the fuselage. In 2006–2007, the aeroplane flew with the first variant of the weapons compartment, the covers of which were metal and fixed; they could only be opened and closed on the ground. The aircraft made about 70 open-bay flights in various ranges, also at supersonic speed. Inside the bay, mock-ups of K-77M air-to-air missiles were hung. Then, in 2008–2009, the target variant of the bay was set up with an improved shape and refined deflectors improving the air flow inside and near the bay, as well as with movable composite covers.

By the end of the test programme in 2010, the experimental Su-47 made a total of about 350 flights. Because of its new purpose, after 2005, Su-47 was not shown to the public for many years. It did not appear until August 2019 at the MAKS exhibition in the group of historical exhibits.

Sukhoi Su-47 Specifications (estimated)

Wingspan	16.7m
Length	22.6m
Height	5.67m
Nominal take-off weight	26,900kg
Maximum take-off weight	35,000kg
Maximum speed	Mach 2.0
Supersonic cruising speed	Mach 1.5
Ceiling	20,000m
Maximum range	4,000km

A full-size mock-up of a forward-swept wing Sukhoi S-22 fighter developed in 1983–1988, the first approach to the future Su-47. (Sukhoi)

Su-47 Berkut performed at all MAKS airshows from 1999 to 2005, always making a big impression with its sharp take-off. Later, the Su-47 was assigned to the tests of Su-57's weapon bays and its demonstrations were stopped. (Piotr Butowski)

The Su-47 carries the basic set of weapons inside the fuselage, in the main compartment with dimensions of about 4.5 x 2.2m and a smaller front compartment with a length of 3.8m and a width decreasing from about 1.4m to 0.8m in front. (Piotr Butowski)

This photo shows how big the Su-47 is compared to the Su-30MK heavy fighter. (Piotr Butowski)

An Su-47 Berkut displayed at the MAKS airshow in August 2019 in the group of historical exhibits. The project started out as a pure experiment in 1983–1988, then developed for a while as the next-generation fighter programme, to end up again as an experimental aircraft. (Piotr Butowski)

The Su-47 prototype flew with makeshift D-30F11 engines from MiG-31. The fairings at the tail booms' tips were to house a rear-facing radar and electronic warfare equipment; in the prototype, the longer fairing houses an anti-spin parachute, and the other one is empty. (Piotr Butowski)

Three views of the Sukhoi Su-47 fighter. (Piotr Butowski)

© Piotr Butowski

Chapter 3
PAK FA Competition

I n the mid-1990s it was already clear that neither of the previous projects, Mikoyan 1.42 and Sukhoi S-32, would go into production and service. Both were very heavy and thus very expensive; not forgetting the nominal (i.e. configured for a typical combat mission) take-off weight of the MiG MFI was 28.6 tonnes. A new round of conceptual work on the aircraft codenamed 'LFS' (Lyogkiy Frontovoi Samolyot (light tactical aircraft)) began – which did not mean that it had to be lightweight.

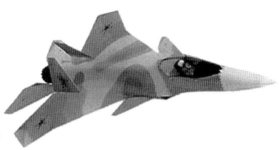

Sukhoi lightweight single-engine fighter concept considered within the LFS programme. (Sukhoi)

The first question to be answered was, should there be one or two new Russian fighters? It is known that the Russians would prefer to have a two-component fleet of fighter aircraft; this was the case with the Su-27 and MiG-29 generations and was to be the case with the MFI and LFI generation. A ratio of one-third heavy fighters to two-thirds light fighters would be the most cost-effective option. In the late 1990s, the idea was to first make the more commercially promising LFS lightweight fighter, which could also be sold in large numbers overseas, and then build a heavy fighter based on it. The chairman of the Air Force's scientific and technical committee, Major General Sergey Kolyadin, said in an interview for *Krasnaya Zvezda* newspaper on 17 March 2000 that 'the complex of technical and technological solutions [obtained in the process of creating a new light fighter] will ensure the creation of a future heavy multi-role fighter for replacing the Su-27 and MiG-31'.

The same Sergey Kolyadin told *Krasnaya Zvezda* on 7 February 2002 that 'the two-type composition of the fighter fleet would be optimal for solving the tasks of the Air Force. However, the creation, and most importantly, the purchase in sufficient numbers and the operation of heavy combat aircraft is an expensive pleasure that only rich countries can afford.' It should be remembered that the turn of the 1990s and 2000s was an extremely difficult period for Russia; the country faced economic turbulence and cut its military spending drastically. In 1998, there was a default in Russia – the state proved unable to pay its debts, and the price of oil, the main source of the Russian budget income, was very low.

Therefore, there was more and more inclination towards the concept of only one new generation fighter, which would be a compromise between requirements and price. Around 1999, the new generation fighter programme was codenamed 'PAK FA' (Perspektivnyi Aviatsionnyi Kompleks Frontovoi Aviatsii (Future Air Complex of Tactical Aviation)), or I-21 (Istrebitel (fighter for the 21st century)).

There was also a discussion about whether to postpone this programme. The Air Force had fairly recently received the Su-27 Flanker, still having a large modernisation potential, and was in no hurry to get a new fighter. The industry, on the other hand, was very interested in receiving a large and expensive order quickly. Mikhail Pogosyan argued in the press for accelerating the work on the PAK FA in order not to break the contact between experienced designers, who were still making the Su-27, and young people who had just finished their education, stating that 'if you postpone the start of the PAK FA programme, then the "old" staff will leave and there will be only young people without experience, who will not be able to develop the aeroplane later'. The director of the GosNIIAS aviation systems institute, Yevgeny Fedosov, made an even more dramatic statement in 2001: 'building a next-generation fighter is a matter of life and death for the Russian aviation industry.'

Fighter projects of the late 1990s

Several of the LFS light fighter designs under consideration were leaked into the public domain. The Sukhoi light fighter design had one AL-41F engine of an enhanced 20-tonne thrust version with a moving three-dimensional thrust vector, as well as a tandem triplane (canard foreplanes, wing and tailplanes) aerodynamic configuration. The head of the acquisitions department in the Russian Armed Forces, Anatoly Sitnov, declared then that the Lyulka-Saturn AL-41F engine would be the base engine for Russian combat aircraft in the near future and would be used both in the lightweight LFS, the following heavy fighter, as well as the Su-27IB fighter-bomber (today's Su-34). Another sketch of the Sukhoi project, published in 2001, showed the aircraft in a classic aerodynamic layout with a trapezoidal wing, two engines and twin tailfins; something similar to the Su-47 Berkut but with a regular wing.

Mikhail Korzhuyev, the then general designer of OKB Mikoyan, said in Farnborough in September 1998 that his team was analysing single- and twin-engine LFS variants, finally stopping on a project with a nominal take-off weight of 15 tonnes and two engines with a thrust of about 80kN; both the Russian RD-33/RD-133 and foreign engines for the export version were considered. The assumption was to use an available, proven and reliable engine to reduce the risk, even if it was not the most modern design.

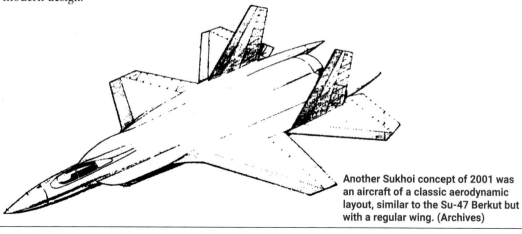

Another Sukhoi concept of 2001 was an aircraft of a classic aerodynamic layout, similar to the Su-47 Berkut but with a regular wing. (Archives)

Finally, in early 2001, it was decided that Russia would have a one fifth-generation fighter to replace both the Su-27 and MiG-29. In April 2001, the Air Force announced a competition for the conceptual design of PAK FA (I-21) and presented the design bureaus with detailed tactical and technical requirements. According to them, the Russian PAK FA was to be placed between the American F-22A and the Joint Strike Fighter. It was supposed to be a multi-role fighter, performing both the tasks of gaining air superiority and attacking surface targets. It was, of course, supposed to achieve supersonic cruising speed, low visibility and short take-off and landing. All the aircraft's avionics, including weapons control, data exchange, electronic warfare, self-defence, communications and navigation systems, were to be combined into an integrated on-board equipment system with a common information field. The PAK FA was intended to carry all Russian air-to-air and tactical air-to-surface missiles, including very long-range munitions.

The original idea of the contest was beautiful. Head of GosNIIAS, Yevgeny Fedosov, at a press conference in Moscow on 19 January 1999, said that the new fighter would be the joint work of three teams: Mikoyan, Sukhoi and Yakovlev. First, everyone would present their own concept, but after selecting one of them, the remaining teams would obtain the status of subcontractors responsible for individual elements of the aircraft. In fact, however, there was a fierce battle around the choice of the

Left: Director of the GosNIIAS aviation systems institute Yevgeny Fedosov: 'Creating the next-generation fighter is a matter of life and death for the Russian aviation industry.' (Piotr Butowski)

Right: The head of the RSK MiG Nikolay Nikitin proposed the creation of a joint consortium for work on the PAK FA fighter. (Piotr Butowski)

main contractor of the PAK FA programme and, as will be seen later, no co-operation between the companies took place.

The first move was made by the Russian Aircraft Corporation (RSK) MiG; since the end of 1999, this is the name of the corporation connecting the Mikoyan design bureau and production plants Voronin in Moscow (currently non-existent), Lukhovitsy and Sokol in Nizhny Novgorod. In April 2001, the then head of the RSK MiG, Nikolay Nikitin, proposed the creation of a joint consortium for work on the PAK FA. It would include Mikoyan, Sukhoi and Yakovlev design teams as well as production plants of Voronin in Moscow, Sokol in Nizhny Novgorod, KnAAPO in Komsomolsk-on-Amur, and IAPO in Irkutsk. In the first stage, design bureaus would prepare conceptual designs for the fighter. The project selected by the state commission would then be developed into a detailed design jointly by all teams, except that most of the work would be done by the winner of the first phase; the others would have a smaller share of the work (and profit). After the prototypes were built and tested, the aircraft would be produced in co-operation with four production plants. This agreement would be a good basis for work on PAK FA, if all interested parties would join it.

All except Sukhoi agreed with the proposal. Such a consortium was inconvenient from the standpoint of Sukhoi's interests. Why share with others when Sukhoi felt it had a good chance of winning the pot itself? In response to the MiG's idea of establishing a consortium, on 18 May 2001, Sukhoi and a group of its business partners, including the Lyulka-Saturn engine design team, the Ramenskoye PKB avionics engineering facility, Aerokosmicheskoye Oborudovaniye (and within its framework the Tikhomirov NIIP radar design facility), the armaments designers of Vympel (air-to-air missiles) and Zvezda-Strela (air-to-ground missiles) signed an agreement for joint work on the next generation's fighter. The research institutes TsAGI (aerodynamics), TsIAM (engines), VIAM (materials), NIAT (technologies) and GosNIIAS (systems integration) also participated in the agreement. Mikhail Pogosyan, General Director of the Sukhoi group, emphasised that the document was open to other participants. The advantage of this agreement was that it covered the entire chain of co-operation – not only the aircraft design and production facilities, but also scientific institutions and producers of avionics and weapons.

Competing concepts

Two projects entered the competition. Sukhoi submitted the T-50 aircraft with two Lyulka AL-41F1 turbofan engines, each with 14.5 tonnes of thrust. Further data is not known, but the projected normal take-off weight can be estimated at 22–23 tonnes, and the maximum weight at 28–30 tonnes.

Normal take-off weight is the weight of an aircraft with full internal fuel and weapons for most typical missions, in this case, four medium-range and two short-range air-to-air missiles.

Mikoyan submitted the E-721 design, made in a layout similar to 1.42, but with smaller dimensions, powered by two Klimov VK-10M engines for about 10–11 tonnes of thrust. Its normal take-off weight can be estimated at 16–17 tonnes. A third Russian fighter designer, Yakovlev, participated in both projects as the subcontractor for the short take-off and vertical landing module planned for the future. Yakovlev has made the Yak-38 and Yak-41 VTOL fighters and the Yak-43 project in the past. By the way, Yakovlev continues his conceptual work on this subject to this day. The IAPO plant in Irkutsk presented its own offer, which believed that the next-generation fighter could be the Su-30 manufactured in Irkutsk with deeply modernised equipment – but it was not serious.

At the MAKS exhibition in August 2001 in Zhukovsky, prototypes of engines for fighters participating in the I-21 (PAK FA) competition were shown. Lyulka-Saturn deployed the AL-41F (izdeliye 20) engine from MiG 1.44. No information was given about it, apart from a general comparison with the 'previous generation engines' (one can guess that these were RD-33 from MiG-29 and AL-31F from Su-27), according to which, the unit weight of the engine had been reduced by 15% and the specific fuel consumption by 10–13%, while the total cost of the engine life cycle was twice as low as before. The Sukhoi T-50 fighter was designed with the AL-41F1 (izdeliye 117) engine, which was a deeply modernised AL-31FP (izdeliye 96) using the AL-41F (izdeliye 20) engine technology.

Klimov from St Petersburg showed the RD-33-10M engine, which was a deep upgrade of the RD-33 and a prototype for the VK-10M engine intended for the PAK FA E-721 designed by MiG. The RD-33-10M engine had a 3-stage fan (instead of four on the RD-33), a slightly modified high-pressure compressor, new turbine blades, digital automation; the turbine entry temperature increased by 10–15%. At the first stage, a maximum thrust of 103kN was planned, and ultimately the VK-10M was to provide a thrust of 118kN. The RD-33-10M engine had a movable nozzle of Klimov's own design, called Klivt (Klimov's vectored thrust), tilted 15° in any direction.

Sukhoi's and Mikoyan's projects corresponded to two different philosophies. Sukhoi proposed a 'maximum capability' fighter in the upper middle class, while MiG proposed a 'minimum essential' at a reasonable price. At MAKS 2001, the management of RSK MiG at a press conference strongly criticised

The general shape of the PAK FA has been known since spring 2007, when its image was briefly displayed on the website of the NPO Saturn engine company. The real aircraft differs from that drawing in the most important element of the aerodynamic configuration: it has large movable front flaps, which are lacking on the picture from 2007. The 'leaked' drawing was probably deliberate disinformation. (NPO Saturn)

Left: The head of OKB MiG Design Bureau Vladimir Barkovsky: 'Our project is a borderline one: lighter would be ineffective, and heavier – too expensive.' (Piotr Butowski)

Right: Major General Sergey Kolyadin: 'Sukhoi's concept was better according to the whole complex of criteria.' (Piotr Butowski)

the 'other project' (without mentioning the name of Sukhoi), which is 'ruining the country's economy'. RSK MiG performed more actively and aggressively, as Sukhoi had been anointed the winner of the competition much earlier in many official statements.

According to MiG, the next-generation fighter had to be cheap enough for the Russian Air Force to buy the necessary number of aircraft with the money available. The adoption of the Sukhoi project would lead to a situation where the Russian Air Force would not be able to afford the purchase of aircraft, and the entire programme would turn out to be a waste of money. The head of the RSK MiG, Nikolai Nikitin, stated that $1.3 billion per year in 2010–25 would be enough to purchase and operate the necessary number of aircraft according to the MiG project, while the heavier Sukhoi aircraft would cost $2 billion a year. Vladimir Barkovsky, deputy director of RSK MiG and the head of the Mikoyan design bureau, said that 'our project is a borderline one: lighter would be ineffective, and heavier – too expensive'.

On 26 April 2002, the government commission selected the Sukhoi T-50 project for the new I-21 (PAK FA) fighter. The decision was made by a government military-industrial commission chaired by the then-Prime Minister Mikhail Kasyanov and not by an Air Force commission. The military themselves tried to transfer the decision to a higher level, wanting to avoid possible criticism and pressure. The already mentioned Major General Sergey Kolyadin, chairman of the military-scientific committee of the Russian Air Force, said at a press conference during the ILA Berlin exhibition in May 2002 that Sukhoi won because 'its concept was better according to a whole complex of criteria'. When making the selection, the experience of Sukhoi's team was also taken into account; in the previous decade, Sukhoi worked with the greatest workload of all teams in Russia, developing the Su-27 fighter into a family of Su-27M and Su-30MKI multi-role fighters, the Su-33 ship-borne fighter and the Su-34 fighter-bomber. The financial stability of Sukhoi, who had a large and steady income from the sale of fighters to China and India, was also important. Sukhoi's fighters were then half of the Russian aviation production and almost half of all exports of military equipment.

The competition was conducted at the level of conceptual designs. A more advanced preliminary design of the PAK FA was to be prepared by the end of 2003 (in fact it was ready at the end of 2004), 'after which a decision will be made on further work', said Kolyadin. He emphasised several times that the most important element for the successful implementation of the PAK FA programme was 'the concentration of the technical, production and financial resources of the entire aviation industry'. According to numerous public declarations submitted by various officials at that time, the first prototype of the fighter was to start flight tests in 2006, and serial production was to start in 2010.

Chapter 4
Sukhoi T-50 Under Development

On 21 July 2003, Sukhoi received a formal contract from the Russian MoD for the research and development (R&D) work (Opytno-Konstruktorskaya Rabota or OKR) codenamed 'Stolitsa-1' (capital city), covering design, construction and tests of the T-50 fighter prototypes. In October 2004, Sukhoi introduced the preliminary design of the T-50 fighter to the Air Force, and this was approved two months later on 10 December 2004. Along with the design, the state commission adopted a plan for further work in the PAK FA programme. In 2005 and 2006, the detailed designing of the aircraft and its equipment continued. Sukhoi developed a computer model of the aircraft and a working model of the cockpit. Alexander Davidenko became the programme director and the chief designer of the T-50 fighter in the Sukhoi design bureau in 2002; in 2014, he was replaced by Mikhail Strelets.

Initially, the project was developed almost exclusively with Sukhoi's own, and its partners', funds; the MoD contributed only 20%. It was only since 2006 (i.e. when the really large expenses began) that most of the financing was taken over by the state in the form of the Ministry of Industry and Energy and the MoD. According to Valery Bezverhhniy, responsible for the formation of the UAC, the financing of the PAK FA programme in 2006 increased 'several times' compared to 2005. According to earlier assumptions, RSK MiG was to be involved in designing the PAK FA. Sukhoi sent an offer to participate in the development of the aircraft to MiG. However, the offer was for such a small level of involvement – MiG would do the empennage and a few smaller components – that RSK MiG did not accept this proposal and took up its own projects: the MiG-29K and MiG-29M/MiG-35 fighters.

The shape of the T-50 was formally frozen with the approval of the preliminary design in December 2004, but changes were still made, even quite significant ones. In January 2006, the Commander-in-

Left: Alexander Davidenko was the head of the Su-57 development programme between 2002 and 2014. (Sukhoi)

Right: Mikhail Strelets is the head of the Sukhoi design bureau and the Su-57 chief designer since 2014. (Piotr Butowski)

Chief of the Russian Air Force, General Vladimir Mikhailov, made a strange statement saying that he had 'ordered a reduction in the maximum speed of the aircraft from Mach 2.15 to Mach 2.0', making the aircraft simpler 'without reducing its combat effectiveness'. A month later, Sukhoi's CEO Mikhail Pogosyan confirmed that 'there is a need to optimize the requirements for PAK FA', including reducing the top speed to Mach 2.

After Sukhoi was selected as the main contractor for the PAK FA programme, further tenders for the construction of the aircraft's main systems were launched. In most cases, Sukhoi chose its traditional partners. One of the few changes was the selection of the on-board equipment system integrator; Sukhoi kept this task to itself although the RPKB company from Ramenskoye had done it for years in Su fighters. In April 2004, Sukhoi signed a contract with Lyulka-Saturn to develop the AL-41F1 (izdielije 117) engine for PAK FA. The MIRES

Mikhail Pogosyan, the head of Sukhoi Group at the time when the Su-57 was being created and now the rector of Moscow Aviation Institute. (Piotr Butowski)

(Sh121) radio-electronic suite including the radar had been ordered in 2003 at the Tikhomirov NIIP institute from Zhukovsky, previously making all radars for Su-27 family fighters. The L402 electronic intelligence and electronic countermeasures suite had been ordered at KNIRTI institute in Zhukov near Kaluga. The order for the OEIS (101KS) electro-optical suite was placed at UOMZ in Yekaterinburg. The new K-36D-5 ejection seat and the pilot's flying suit were ordered from Zvezda in Tomilino. New internal-carriage weapons for PAK FA were ordered from companies belonging to the Tactical Missiles Corporation (KTRV).

The construction of the T-50 prototypes was launched by the Sukhoi-KnAAZ plant in Komsomolsk-on-Amur in the Russian far east. The prototype was not made at the Sukhoi workshop in Moscow, which was previously the norm in the USSR. The Komsomolsk plant is now formally called the Branch of Public Joint Stock Company Aviation Holding Sukhoi – Komsomolsk-on-Amur Aviation Plant, named after Yuri Gagarin, abbreviated to Sukhoi-KnAAZ. In the past, starting in 1936, the plant produced, among others, DB-3 (Il-4) bombers, Li-2 (DC-3) transport aircraft; MiG-15 and MiG-17 fighters; and from 1957, Sukhoi aircraft including Su-7, Su-17, Su-20 and Su-22 Fitter fighter-bombers; and since 1984, the Flanker family fighters Su-27, Su-30, Su-33 and Su-35. The current production is Su-35 and Su-57 as well as elements for the SSJ100 Superjet regional passenger jet.

First flight of T-50-1

On 29 January 2010, the first prototype T-50-1 performed its maiden flight from the factory airfield in Komsomolsk-on-Amur; the test pilot Sergey Bogdan was at the controls. The flight lasted 47 minutes and, according to Sukhoi's statement, 'went smoothly, completely as scheduled'. During the flight, a preliminary assessment of the aircraft's controllability, engine operation and basic installations was made; the aircraft retracted and extended the landing gear twice. 'The airplane worked properly in all flight phases. It is easy and convenient to pilot', added Sergey Bogdan. Earlier, on 21 January 2010, the T-50-1 made its first high-speed taxi run. On 12 February 2010, the T-50-1 completed its second flight, which lasted 57 minutes, and on 13 February, its third one. A few weeks later, on 8 April 2010, the T-50-1 (along with the T-50-KNS, described below) was transported on board An-124 to the Sukhoi's flight test base in Zhukovsky near Moscow; the only location with the necessary infrastructure for advanced aircraft trials.

The T-50-1 is used for flight handling evaluation and has no mission systems. After more than a year of testing, on 9 March 2011, it exceeded the speed of sound for the first time. In summer

The first prototype of the Su-57, the T-50-1, being prepared for its maiden flight at the frosty Komsomolsk-on-Amur airfield in Russia's far east. (Sukhoi)

2011, an anti-spin parachute was installed inside the aircraft's tail cone. On 13 June 2013, Russian television reported on the 'conclusion of an important stage of trials' of the T-50 fighter. During the accompanying footage, the T-50-1 was shown completing a flat spin.

The first public display of the T-50 took place at Moscow's International Aviation and Space Salon (MAKS) exhibition in August 2011, where both the T-50-1 and T-50-2 flying at that time performed. The aircraft could only be seen from a distance in flight; when on the ground, they were covered with large tilts.

Initially, the T-50-1 was numbered 51; in 2012, the number was changed to 051 as it is today. In 2018, especially for the Victory Day parade on 9 May 2018, the aircraft received a new pixel painting; the same livery was given to almost all other T-50s. The T-50-1 is still used for tests in Zhukovsky and Akhtubinsk.

Three non-flying T-50s were built and are intended for various types of ground tests. The most interesting of them is the T-50-KNS (Kompleksnyi Naturnyi Stend (complex full-scale stand)) mock-up intended for on-ground synchronisation of all construction components. On 23 December 2009, even before the first flight of the T-50-1, the T-50-KNS performed taxiing on the runway in Komsomolsk-on-Amur, which was watched by the invited Indian delegation. Since April 2010, T-50-KNS has been located in Zhukovsky, where it is still being used to 'try on' new elements of structures and equipment. In August 2019, this particular aeroplane, with the number '057', was publicly shown at MAKS 2019 as the export Su-57E. A year later, the T-50-KNS was shown at the Army 2020 exhibition in Kubinka with next-generation 'izdeliye 30' engine mock-ups.

Two more non-flying specimens are intended for static stress tests. The first T-50-0 was made in Komsomolsk and on 29 October 2009, it was delivered to the Sukhoi design bureau in Moscow. In December 2014, it was joined by T-50-7, made according to the 'second-stage' project.

The T-50's maiden flight on 29 January 2010. (Sukhoi)

Sukhoi's chief test pilot Sergey Bogdan and the company's head Mikhail Pogosyan just after the T-50's maiden flight. (Sukhoi)

Left: One of the first T-50-1 flights made in Zhukovsky; the aircraft still has a standard tail cone. (Piotr Butowski)

Below: Disassembled T-50-1 in April 2010 when transported on board An-124 to continue flight trials at the Sukhoi's flight test base in Zhukovsky near Moscow. (Sukhoi)

The first public demonstration of the T-50-1 at the MAKS 2011 airshow. During a display on 17 August 2011, the aircraft suffered a structural crack, even flying with the g-load limited to 5. The repairs took more than a year; the T-50-1 resumed flight tests in September 2012. Note an anti-spin parachute at the long fuselage tail cone. (Piotr Butowski)

The same T-50-1 performed at MAKS 2019 in a new pixelated livery applied to most Su-57 aircraft in spring 2018. (Piotr Butowski)

The 'zero' example of Su-57, the T-50-0 prototype, serves at the Sukhoi design bureau in Moscow for static stress and fatigue tests. (Sukhoi)

T-50-2

The second flying prototype T-50-2 made its first flight on 3 March 2011; initially numbered '52', in 2012 it changed to '052'. Like the first prototype, the T-50-2 has no mission systems and has therefore been used for tests of aircraft's basic systems, including the weapon bay door actuating mechanism, aerial refuelling and others. On 3 August 2012, it made its first 'dry' aerial contact with an Il-78 tanker. The fuel receiver on the T-50 is pulled out from under the cover on the left side in front of the pilot's cockpit. Measurement lines were painted on the nose of the T-50-2 to analyse the recording of the refuelling operation. In total in this test cycle, the T-50-2 made contact with the Il-78 tanker 17 times; fuel was transferred three times.

In the first half of 2013, the T-50-2 was strengthened and adapted for attaining high g-loads and angles of attack. In 2017, the aircraft had been converted into T-50-2LL (Letayushchaya Laboratoriya (flying testbed)) with the port engine replaced by a prototype of the 'izdeliye 30' next-generation engine.

The second T-50-2 performed its first flight on 3 March 2011. (Sukhoi)

Left and above: Between December 2012 and May 2013, the T-50-2 prototype underwent modernisation in the Sukhoi workshops in Moscow. The aircraft structure has been strengthened; many new overlays have appeared on the surface of the airframe. (Piotr Butowski)

The T-50-2 approaches landing presenting a flat bottom of the fuselage housing two large weapon bays. (Piotr Butowski)

At MAKS 2011, the T-50 could only be seen from a distance in flight; when on the ground, the aircraft was covered with large tilt. (Piotr Butowski)

The T-50-2 performs during the celebration of the 100th anniversary of the Russian Air Force in Zhukovsky in August 2012. In the background you can see a Curtiss P-40N Kittyhawk and a North American P-51D Mustang, World War Two fighters invited to this event. (Piotr Butowski)

Above and right: Sharp take-off of the T-50-2 prototype during the Russian Air Force's 100th anniversary show in August 2012. Measurement lines were painted on the aircraft nose to analyse the recording of the aerial refuelling operation. (Piotr Butowski)

MAKS airshow in Zhukovsky in August 2011. That was a time when military aircraft from the West participated in airshows in Russia. Here, the US Air Force McDonnell Douglas F-15E Strike Eagle is visible behind the Sukhoi T-50-2 approaching landing. (Piotr Butowski)

Left: Sukhoi T-50-2 leaves the Zhukovsky airfield in 2013. (Piotr Butowski)

Below: Sukhoi T-50-2 approaches landing at the MAKS 2017 airshow. (Piotr Butowski)

T-50-3

The T-50-3 made its first flight on 22 November 2011 in Komsomolsk-on-Amur; from the beginning to this day, it has had the same side number '053'. After making several flights in Komsomolsk, it was dismantled and transported to Zhukovsky in December 2011. There, in Sukhoi's workshop, the N036 Byelka radar (in a reduced version with front X-band antenna only) and some sensors of the 101KS Atoll electro-optical suite (including the 101KS-V infrared search and track) were installed on it; it was the first T-50 to receive mission sensors. Beginning on 21 June 2012, initial radar tests were conducted on T-50-3; on 26 July 2012, the radar was switched on for the first time in flight. The T-50-3 features some minor design changes, including slightly different wingtips and differently shaped air intakes in the vertical tail-fin roots. Three UV-50-01 decoy launchers are mounted in the T-50-3's tail boom.

Right: Sergei Bogdan in the T-50-3 cockpit before the first flight on 22 November 2011. (Sukhoi)

Below: First flight of the third T-50-3, 22 November 2011. (Sukhoi)

Above: The T-50-3 is about to land after its first flight on 22 November 2011, assisted with an Su-17 spotter aircraft. (Sukhoi)

Left: T-50-3 is the first Su-57 prototype fitted with the N036 radar (in a reduced version with front X-band antenna only) and part of the 101KS Atoll electro-optical sensors. (Piotr Butowski)

On 26 July 2012, the N036 radar on T-50-3 was switched on in flight for the first time. (Piotr Butowski)

In 2019, the T-50-3 was converted into a testbed for testing the automatic take-off and landing system for the S-70 Okhotnik unmanned aircraft. Along with this, the aeroplane was painted in the likeness of the Okhotnik.

T-50-4

The T-50-4 (number '054') took off for the first time in Komsomolsk-on-Amur on 12 December 2012. On 15–17 January 2013, the T-50-4 flew 7,000km from Komsomolsk to Zhukovsky on its own; the previous aircraft were transported from Komsomolsk to Zhukovsky on an An-124 airlifter. The T-50-4 has been equipped with the N036 Byelka radar for the first time during production in Komsomolsk-on-Amur, and later in Zhukovsky. It is also the first of the T-50 prototypes to receive the L402 Himalaya electronic warfare system.

Changes also took place in the completion of the 101KS Atoll electro-optical suite. On the sides of the T-50-4 fuselage, just behind the pilot's cockpit, two sensors of the 101KS-U ultraviolet missile approach warning system were installed for the first time. Together with two other 101KS-U sensors (first installed on the T-50-3 aircraft) under the front of the fuselage and on the top of the tail beam, the system now provides coverage of the entire space around the aircraft.

Sergey Bogdan in the T-50-4 cockpit before the first flight on 12 December 2012. The 101KS-V optical-sight turret is fitted in front of the cockpit, and the 101KS-U ultraviolet warning sensor is behind it. A 30mm cannon is embedded in the fuselage side below. (Sukhoi)

The T-50-4 ready for departure from Komsomolsk-on-Amur to Zhukovsky in January 2013. It was the first of the T-50 prototypes to complete this 7,000km route on its own. (Sukhoi)

Left and below: T-50-4 is the first of the Su-57 prototypes to receive the full set of four 101KS-U ultraviolet missile approach warning sensors that provide a coverage of the entire space around the aircraft, as well as the L402 Himalaya electronic warfare system. (Piotr Butowski)

Right and below: The T-50-4 continues test flights; here it is in a new 2018 livery. (Piotr Butowski)

T-50-5

The last test aircraft from the first batch, the T-50-5 ('055'), took off for the first time on 27 October 2013; like all previous prototypes, it was flown by Sergei Bogdan. The T-50-5 had a differently configured 101KS Atoll system lacking 101KS-U warning sensors but featuring two (previously there was one) 101KS-O EO turrets, including the sensor mounted under the forward fuselage.

The T-50-5 received a new camouflage scheme, with dark grey upper surfaces and light grey below, with an indistinct demarcation between them. Later, after the repair described below, the T-50-5R was painted in a similar fashion, but with a sharp border between the colours; finally in spring 2018 it received the pixel paint scheme, which is now standard for Su-57 prototypes.

Above and below: The T-50-5 ('055'), that took off for the first time on 27 October 2013, is the last test aircraft of the first batch. (Piotr Butowski)

The T-50-5 caught fire on the runway in Zhukovsky after landing on 10 June 2014. (Sukhoi)

Right: The fifth aircraft, designated T-50-5R after the repair, resumed the flight tests in October 2015. (Sukhoi)

Below left and below right: In spring 2018, the T-50-5R was given the pixel painting, which is now standard for Su-57 prototypes. (Piotr Butowski)

Tests on other aircraft

In addition to the five T-50 prototypes, three experimental aircraft using other platforms participated in the PAK FA programme flights. The internal weapons compartment was tested on the Su-47 fighter. The new KSU-50 flight control system for the T-50 was tested on the Su-27M '708' fighter. The AL-41F1 engine was tested on the Su-27M '710' aircraft. By February 2014, a total of 275 test flights had been carried out on them.

The Su-27M '710' fighter served as a flying test bed for trials of the AL-41F1 engine, which was fitted at starboard nacelle. The second engine remained the standard AL-31F. (Piotr Butowski)

One of the emergency landings, this time in August 2011. The T-50-1 comes in to land after a failure of the starboard engine and an emergency fuel dump. (Piotr Butowski)

Summary of the first stage of trials

In February 2014, Sukhoi summarised the first cycle of preliminary trials, PI-1. By that time, five T-50 prototypes had completed 402 flights (the 500th flight of a T-50 was performed by Yuri Vashchuk on 14 August 2014). During the tests, the aircraft reached the maximum Mach number of 1.7, the instrument speed of 1,000km/h (including 800km/h with open weapon bays), the ceiling of 14,000m and the g-load of +6/-2 in subsonic flight and +4 in supersonic flight. The properties in flight at critical angles of attack 'exceeded the results of the fourth generation airplanes' and the achieved low-visibility characteristics 'met the tactical and technical requirements'. Phase two of the preliminary trials, PI-2, ran from 2014 to 2019; in parallel, the aircraft participated in state trials (see page 46).

The trials of the first five T-50 prototypes were accompanied by problems with the strength of the airframe, which were initially addressed with various strengthening additions on the T-50 airframes, and which eventually led to a deeper reworking of the design of subsequent aircraft. During the MAKS 2011 demonstration flight on 17 August 2011, the T-50-1 suffered a structural crack, even flying with the g-load limited to 5; further problems were revealed when dismantling the airframe. The inspection of the structure and the application of reinforcements took more than a year; the T-50-1 resumed flight tests in Zhukovsky on 11 September, 2012.

On several occasions, the aircraft have suffered engine problems and have landed with one engine shut down. On 21 August 2011, the T-50-2 encountered a compressor stall of the starboard engine during a take-off roll; a flame several metres long extended from the exhaust nozzle and the aircraft aborted the take-off. On 10 April 2015, during a test flight of another T-50, the canopy glazing cracked at an altitude of 4,500m; pilot Sergey Bogdan landed safely.

The fifth aircraft, T-50-5, suffered the most when it caught fire on the runway in Zhukovsky after landing on 10 June 2014, unluckily during a presentation for an Indian delegation. The overhaul at Komsomolsk-on-Amur lasted 16 months; on 16 October 2015, the aircraft, now designated T-50-5R, resumed flight tests after repair.

Military aircraft test procedures in Russia

Tests of military aircraft in Russia are divided into several stages. The first stage consists of preliminary trials (Predvaritelnye Ispytaniya (PI)) conducted by the aircraft's manufacturer at the Gromov Flight Research Institute (LII) at Zhukovsky near Moscow.

After the successful completion of preliminary trials – which check the aircraft's basic performance and flight handling, and ensure their compliance with the Russian Aerospace Forces requirements – the aircraft is handed over for joint state trials (Gosudarstvennye Sovmestnye Ispytaniya (GSI)) conducted at the 929th Chkalov State Flight Test Centre (Gosudarstvennyi lyotno-ispytatelnyi tcentr imeni V.P. Chkalova (GLITs)) in the MoD at Akhtubinsk. The first stage of state trials, GSI-1, concludes with the acceptance of the aircraft as a flying vehicle. During the second stage, GSI-2, mission systems and armaments are tested.

Chapter 5

The Second Five with Stronger Airframe

At the very beginning of the programme, it was planned to use four to six test aircraft; then serial production of the fighter was to start. However, problems with insufficient structural strength caused these plans to change. With strengthening overlays and local corrections on the T-50-1 to -5 aircraft, these problems could only be fixed temporarily. For further progress on the PAK FA programme to be made, more significant changes to the airframe structure of the aircraft were needed, and another batch of five prototypes (plus one static) made according to the corrected design were built to test them. There is no official information on this subject, but one can be sure that the strengthening of the structure increased its weight and thus worsened the performance of the aircraft in relation to what was originally planned.

In October 2012, a decision was made to build another batch of test aircraft according to a revised design called the 'second stage'. Note that the use of the term 'second stage' for strengthened-structure aircraft is somewhat misleading; in fact, the second stage of the PAK FA programme was to be the Su-57M aircraft, now under development, with new 'izdeliye 30' engines.

The first of the reinforced aircraft was the T-50-7, an airframe intended for static stress tests; it was brought from Komsomolsk to Moscow in December 2014. In February 2015, the UAC announced in a press release that, 'in 2015, three more flying prototypes should join the test programme'. In fact, the first flight prototype of the second stage, the T-50-6 '056' made its maiden flight on 27 April 2016, two and a half years after the fifth T-50-5. There is some confusion with the T-50-6 designation. Initially, the T-50-6 was supposed to be the last prototype of the original design. However, it was decided that it was not needed as the aircraft was to be redesigned anyway. Its elements were used to repair the burned T-50-5. Another T-50-6 (called T-50-6-2 for some time) had already been made according to the updated design.

The T-50-6 was followed by T-50-8 '058' (first flight on 17 November 2016), T-50-9 '509' (24 April 2017), T-50-11 '511' (6 August 2017), and T-50-10 '510' (23 December 2017).

The second-stage aircraft differs from the previous examples in having a reinforced inner structure of the airframe. The aft fuselage section (housing the electronic warfare equipment) became longer; the circumferences of the aft lower fuselage, some doors and hatches as well as wingtips have been modified. The wingspan has been increased from 14.0m (45ft 11in) to 14.1m (46ft 3in), and the fuselage length from 19.7m (64ft 7in) to 20.1m (66ft); these are estimated data. Inside, the aircraft received increasingly expanded mission equipment and avionics. The last two aircraft, T-50-10 and T-50-11, are fully equipped; the T-50-11 is a pattern for the series production.

As of the end of 2020, all ten Su-57 prototypes are still flying. While the first five T-50 prototypes are usually tested in Zhukovsky, the second-stage aircraft spend most of their time at the MoD evaluation facility in Akhtubinsk. The MAKS airshow in August and September 2019 was notable, with the first five T-50-1 to T-50-5R aircraft participating, and none of the other five.

T-50 named Su-57

On 18 July 2017, on the first day of the MAKS airshow, the President of Russia Vladimir Putin was to visit a hangar specially prepared for him with the then latest T-50-9 prototype of the PAK FA fighter. It was planned that, in the presence of Putin, a preliminary protocol for the completion of the first stage of tests would be signed there, as well as a recommendation to make an initial series of aircraft, and along with this, the new designation Su-57 would be officially announced. However, because of the delay, Vladimir Putin bypassed the PAK FA hangar, away from the main route of the visit, and the signing of the documents was delayed. Nevertheless, the new designation came into force, and from July 2017 the T-50 fighter was named Su-57.

Parallel to the preliminary tests conducted by Sukhoi at the Russian aviation industry test centre in Zhukovsky, state trials were conducted at the 929 GLITs of the MoD at Akhtubinsk on Volga River, 130 km from Volgograd. In April 2013, the first pilot from outside Sukhoi's team, Rafael Suleymanov from the 929 GLITs centre, made his first flight in a T-50 in Zhukovsky. On 21 February 2014, the T-50-2 prototype was deployed for three months to Akhtubinsk. The purpose was preliminary familiarisation and adaptation of the centre to the upcoming state trials of a completely new system, which was the next-generation fighter.

Formally, the state trials at the 929 GLITs began in December 2014, and the first aircraft to join them was the T-50-3 – the first of the prototypes to be equipped with radar and optical fire-control systems, albeit in reduced variants. However, the formal state test procedures were then halted while waiting for the upgraded T-50 prototypes to arrive. Of course, the older aircraft continued to fly, but only as part of the PI-2 preliminary trials. Gradually, more T-50s followed and joined the tests.

The first stage of state trials, GSI-1, was launched again in 2016 and ended with the signing of a relevant act on 12 May 2018, which formally provided the clearance for production of an initial batch of aircraft. Sukhoi was awarded a contract for such a batch of two aircraft during the Army exhibition in Kubinka in August 2018.

The first GSI-1 stage of the state trials was actually not a very advanced level of readiness; its successful completion means acceptance of the aircraft as a platform. Only the completion of the second GSI-2 stage, when mission systems and armament are tested, provides the clearance for operational service. The GSI-2 started in 2018, with completion planned first in 2019 and then in 2020.

In early May 2020, Russia's Deputy Prime Minister responsible for the arms industry, Yuri Borisov, gave an interview to the Russian press in which he announced that the state trials programme for the new

During MAKS 2017, a separate hangar was set up for the T-50-9 prototype, painted in a pixelated camouflage pattern, which was the same as that of the aircraft. There, the fighter was to be shown to Vladimir Putin and was to be officially named Su-57. However, Putin was late and did not enter the hangar; there was no ceremony, and the aircraft received the new name without publicity. (Piotr Butowski)

Above and below: The T-50-9 prototype being prepared to be presented to Vladimir Putin during the MAKS 2017 airshow. (Piotr Butowski)

On 21 February 2014, the T-50-2 prototype was deployed to the 929th GLITs in Akhtubinsk for preliminary familiarisation; state trials started there in December 2014. (Russia's MoD)

Left: Su-57 '058' in a test flight in Akhtubinsk with the cockpit's canopy removed. (Russia's MoD)

Below: Starting in 2016, the Su-57 prototypes spend most of their time at the Akhtubinsk military test facility, where they undergo acceptance trials. This time there were eight of them together. (Russia's MoD)

Bottom: Su-57 fighters undergo acceptance trials at the Akhtubinsk 929th GLITs. (Russia's MoD)

Su-57 fighter 'has entered its final phase. More than 3,500 flights have already been performed. The Su-57 confirmed almost all the requirements of the tactical and technical specifications in full', he said ('almost all in full' demonstrates the intricacies of the Russian bureaucratic language). In 2020, the first aircraft was to be delivered to the Aerospace Forces, and then, 'it is planned to significantly increase the volumes' of the production.

Deployment to Syria

In February 2018, two prototypes, T-50-9 and T-50-11 were deployed to Syria for a very brief two-day evaluation. On 25 May 2018, at a meeting of a board of Russia's MoD, the Russian Minister of Defence Sergey Shoygu declared that, 'for an assessment in combat conditions of the declared capabilities of the developed military equipment, in February of this year, practical launches of advanced theatre – and tactical level cruise missiles from the 5th generation Su-57 fighter were carried out'. Poor-quality footage accompanying the speech showed the release of a large, more than 4m long, missile from the aft internal weapon bay of Su-57. After one to two seconds of free fall, the missile's wing was extended and the engine in its body was launched. Among known Russian airborne missiles, this missile was most similar to the Raduga Kh-69.

Shoygu spoke and showed the video of the missile launch in the context of the deployment of fighters to Syria. However, if you read his words carefully, he did not explicitly state that these particular launches were performed in Syria. It is very doubtful that the launch of the Kh-69 took place in Syria, especially since the fired missile in the video is red in colour and that is peculiar for an experimental weapon used in range tests.

Many months later, in November 2018, the Russian MoD published footage showing two aircraft taking off and landing at Hmeimim air base in Syria; their tactical numbers were painted over, but the camouflage scheme indicated '509' and '511'. They were assigned registrations especially for

Right and below: Su-57 '509' and '511' when deployed to Syria in February 2018. Note that the aircraft had no corner reflectors that should hide the actual radar cross section. (Russia's MoD)

the international overflight: the '511' became RF-81755; the other registration is unknown. The commentary on the video said, 'the aircraft technical characteristics, the intellectual data management and indication system, the activity of all on-board systems including the weapons, were checked in real conditions of increased temperatures, complex ground surface and other factors. The Su-57 crews performed more than ten flights in Syria.' This means that the Su-57s were using their weapons in Syria although it is very doubtful that these were the new Kh-69 missiles. At the same time, the footage confirmed earlier rumours that the Su-57s flew there without corner reflectors which is what enabled those who observed them in the skies over Syria to learn their radar signature.

The purpose of this short Su-57 trip to Syria remains unclear. It is rather doubtful that this was a trial, as there is not much that can be done in two days. Attention should also be paid to the dates: the fighters were in Syria between 22 and 24 February 2018. Meanwhile, 23 February is Defender of the Fatherland Day in Russia (formerly the Day of the Soviet Army), one of the biggest national holidays. As for the trials, the aircraft would have arrived in Syria after the holiday, which is a day off in Russia. One of the possible explanations is the loud state-of-the-nation speech delivered by Vladimir Putin a week later, on 1 March 2018, when he presented the new kinds of Russian arms, including the Kinzhal airborne missile system and the nuclear-powered Burevestnik cruise missile. It is possible that other subjects, including a film about the Su-57's deployment to Syria, were also being prepared for the speech. However, this subject was not chosen for the final version of the presentation.

The Russian press reported that the Su-57s were used in Syria again later, but there have been no details or confirmation of this news.

On 9 May 2018, a pair of Su-57 fighters flew for the first time in the Victory Day parade over the Red Square in Moscow. The T-50-4 and T-50-5R prototypes, piloted by Taras Artsebarsky and Andrei Shendrik, Sukhoi's test pilots, flew in the tactical aircraft column. They took off from their permanent base in Zhukovsky, belonging to the aviation industry and not to the MoD. Formally, they were the only civilian aircraft participating in the parade. The fighters received new pixel painting especially for the parade, which was later adopted for most of the other Su-57s. Two years later, on 9 May 2020, four Su-57 fighters participated in the parade.

On 9 May 2018, a pair of Su-57 fighters, T-50-4 and T-50-5R prototypes, flew for the first time in the Victory Day parade over the Red Square in Moscow. (Piotr Butowski)

Above: Two years later, on 9 May 2020, four Su-57 fighters participated in the parade over Moscow. (Russia's MoD)

Right: Su-57 in its original paint scheme. (Piotr Butowski)

In 2018–2020, Su-57 aircraft were repainted in a new pattern with large pixels. (Russia's MoD)

The T-50-6 '056', made according to a revised design, performed its maiden flight on 27 April 2016, two and a half years after the fifth T-50-5. (Sukhoi)

Another five prototypes – the T-50-8 is seen here – have a strengthened internal structure. (Piotr Butowski)

The T-50-11 '511'performed its first flight on 6 August 2017. It is considered by Sukhoi as a final model for serial production. (Sukhoi)

The latest prototypes, including this T-50-11, differ from the previous examples in having a reinforced inner structure and a full configuration of mission equipment and avionics.

Chapter 6
The Indian Saga

From the very beginning of the PAK FA programme, the Russians were actively considering the participation of a foreign partner in the programme. The main reason was the desire to attract additional money to this project at the R&D stage and then have a guaranteed large client. The main obstacle was the position of the Russian military, who believed that the Russian aviation industry was already overly foreign orientated. Not forgetting that the then most modern Russian Su-30MKI fighter was produced for India, not for Russia.

According to the government's *United Aircraft Corporation Concept* document, released on 28 October 2004, the PAK FA should be transformed into an international project in which 'Russia will retain its leadership and integrator position'. Foreign investment and technology should be attracted to the programme. China could be a strategic partner, but this would pose a high geopolitical risk for Russia. There are currently good Sino-Russian relations, but until quite recently, almost until the end of the 1980s, they were cold and even earlier – hostile. A much safer partner would be India, which has been buying and producing Russian military aircraft under license for decades.

For the first time, common Russian–Indian next-generation fighters became the subject of talks in June of 2001 in Moscow. Later on, during the visit of the then Indian Defence Minister George Fernandez to Moscow in January 2003, Russia and India signed the letter of intention of common development of the new generation fighter.

The next Indian Defence Minister, Pranab Mukherjee, during his visit to Moscow in November 2005, became acquainted with both the Sukhoi T-50 and MiG E-721 projects. Immediately afterwards, the minister stated that India did not want to be just a source of money: 'Our Air Force and industry wish participation in all stages of development of the new generation fighter, starting from concept definition, through design and tests all the way to series production.' Mukherjee did not name specific companies or projects, but the phrase above clearly infers a preference for the MiG fighter. Sukhoi's project had already taken shape then and the documentation for the construction of prototypes was being completed. What's more, it was built according to the requirements of the Russian Air Force and did not take into account Indian requirements.

Nevertheless, Russia continued to push for India to join the Sukhoi T-50 programme. In early August 2006, Sukhoi's delegation was again in India and presented its project to the MoD. Finally, on 18 October 2007, during a visit to Moscow by Indian Defence Minister, A K Antony, Russia and India signed an inter-governmental agreement (IGA) regarding the common development of the Prospective Multifunction Fighter (PMF), in India commonly named the Fifth-Generation Fighter Aircraft (FGFA), based on the Sukhoi T-50 design. The IGA was followed by a general contract in December 2008, which detailed the workshare and costs. Both sides were to equally finance the project as well as design and produce it together. The head of Sukhoi, Mikhail Pogosyan, explained that the 50:50 parity in the programme, 'will be achieved throughout the life cycle of the aircraft'. As the T-50 project was already very advanced, it was difficult to expect equal participation of India in the design and testing phase; India would have to adapt the aircraft to the requirements of its own Air Force and third countries and then modernise and maintain the fighter for several decades. In this way, on average, the parity of the participation of both parties would be obtained. However, on 6 January 2010, after the first test taxiing of the T-50-KNS in Komsomolsk-on-Amur

Signing a contract covering the preliminary design of the PMF/FGFA to be jointly developed by Sukhoi and HAL, 22 December 2010. (Sukhoi)

in December 2009, which was watched by the Indian delegation, the Indian newspaper *Business Standard* published an article by Ajai Shukla entitled 'India to develop 25% of fifth-generation fighter.' Perhaps the new figure of 25% was the size of India's participation in this programme negotiated in the course of further talks; Sukhoi declined to comment on this article.

On 22 December 2010, when the then Russian President Dmitry Medvedev was in India, a contract was signed covering the preliminary design of the PMF/FGFA, in which each party contributed $295 million. The aircraft was being jointly developed by Sukhoi and HAL of India on the basis of the T-50; it received the codename 'Type 79L'. Within this stage of the work, the aircraft components were being preliminary designed; for example, Tikhomirov NIIP made a design of the N079 radar, this being a Russian–Indian equivalent of the Russian N036 radar. Many systems got export designations with the '79L' index, for example UV-79L flare launchers, RSUO-79L stores management system, etc. In 2012–2013, a group of Indian designers from HAL worked at Sukhoi's headquarters in Moscow. During the Aero India exhibition in Bangalore in February 2013 (and then again in February 2015) in the HAL pavilion, a model of the Russian–Indian new generation PMF/FGFA fighter made in 1:15.5 scale was displayed. It did not differ from the Russian version, except it was in the colours of the Indian Air Force (IAF).

The preliminary design was accepted in June 2013. Russia expected the next contract, worth about $8 billion and covering the construction and evaluation of prototypes, to be signed soon after. The official statement from the Russian UAC in February 2015 said that, 'the Russian and Indian governments have generally agreed on the workshare of each party. The parties have approved the PMF/FGFA specifications, defined their contributions and singled out the systems and subsystems to be developed by India.'

However, subsequent reports from India were increasingly unfavourable and unflattering for PMF/FGFA. In October 2012, the then IAF boss, Air Chief Marshal N A K Browne, announced that the IAF would buy only 144 FGFAs instead of the 214 that was originally planned. According to N A K Browne, the first prototype of the PMF fighter was to be flown by Indian test pilots in 2014; the second one was due in 2017 and the third in 2019. According to a source in the Russian aviation industry, the prototype handed over to India for testing was to be the sixth T-50-6, which was due to take off in the second half of 2013. The launch of production in India was scheduled for 2018–19.

In February 2015, Indian Chief of Air Staff, Air Chief Marshal Arup Raha, said that the quantity of fighters that India would acquire was still undetermined and would depend on financial factors; media

Above and left: A model of the Russian–Indian new generation PMF/FGFA fighter displayed at Aero India 2013. Note the '79L' index. (Piotr Butowski)

reports suggested 127 aircraft, and later, no more than 65 aircraft. Immediately thereafter, the Russian UAC published a counter article in its corporate journal in which publications about the Indian contract reduction were called – indirectly – competitor-inspired disinformation.

The Indian side questioned the technical level of the aircraft and therefore also the need for India to participate in this programme. In January 2014, *Business Standard* quoted a top Indian Air Force official saying that, 'the FGFA's engine is unreliable, its radar inadequate, its stealth features badly engineered, India's workshare too low, and the fighter's price will be exorbitant by the time it enters service.' The IAF demanded some 40–50 improvements to the T-50's design.

India had also complained that its specialists, including pilots, had not been allowed near the aircraft. Russia later argued that the stalemate in the negotiations had been overcome. A UAC report published in June 2016 stated that, 'in the financial matters [the costs of the Indian contribution to research and development work – author's note] a compromise solution has been reached. In the matter of allowing Indian pilots [to fly the PAK FA prototypes] important decisions have been made and they are currently being settled with [the Russian] Ministry of Defence'. According to another UAC report from June 2017, 'the technical negotiations have been concluded', and the contract for full-scale development of the PMF/FGFA 'is initialled and is currently undergoing approval procedures in Indian state authorities'.

Nevertheless, further negotiations stopped and India began to take an even cooler approach to the FGFA programme. Remarkably, in the HAL exhibition hall during Aero India 2017 and 2019 there was no mention of the PMF/FGFA. However, the Indian indigenous Advanced Medium Combat Aircraft (AMCA) was widely advertised. In April 2018, *Business Standard* reported, that the joint Russian–Indian FGFA fighter project had been eventually abandoned.

Above: An Indian Air Force delegation watching T-50 in Zhukovsky on 23 May 2011. From left to right, Air Marshal Vivek Ram Chaudhary, Air Chief Marshal Pradeep Vasant Naik, Mikhail Pogosyan and Pavel Vlasov (head of the Zhukovsky flight test centre). (Sukhoi)

Right: Air Marshal Vivek Ram Chaudhary in the cockpit of T-50-1 prototype on 23 May 2011; Sukhoi test pilot Sergey Bogdan gives an explanation. (Sukhoi)

Chapter 7

Su-57 Acquisition Plans

Today, recalling previous announcements and promises in the Su-57 programme should qualify as bullying. All these assessments were enthusiastic and not very realistic. The Russians particularly underestimated the difficulties that may arise in the course of the trials and believed that the aircraft would be successful right away.

In August 2001, during the MAKS 2001 airshow, the then Commander-in-Chief of the Air Force, Anatoly Kornukov, declared that the new generation PAK FA fighter would take off for the first time in 2006 and would enter service in 2010. In 2006, i.e. when the work on T-50 was already quite advanced, the Russian Defence Minister Sergei Ivanov announced that the first prototype would fly in 2009 (which wasn't far off); deliveries to military units were to start around 2015.

On 1 February 2010, saluting the creators of the T-50 shortly after the fighter's maiden flight, Vladimir Putin, the then Russian Prime Minister, said that in 2013, the first pre-series fighters would be delivered to the Air Force's Crew Conversion Centre at Lipetsk, and by 2015, full-scale production would be launched. The Lipetsk centre is tasked with conducting military evaluations of initial batches of tactical combat aircraft, developing air force tactics and training pilots in combat application of the aircraft.

In December 2012, another Commander-in-Chief of the Russian Air Force, Lieutenant General Viktor Bondarev, announced that, 'sometime in 2015 or at the beginning of 2016, the aircraft should enter the series production' and combat units. In July 2013, under the official *Schedule of activity of the Russia's Ministry of Defence for 2013–2020*, the PAK FA's initial operational capability and the launching of full-scale series production were specified for 31 December 2016. In another document from 2014, Sukhoi gave the 2016 deadline for the implementation of the preliminary batch of fighters and 2018 for the start of mass production.

Opposite and right: On 17 June 2010, Russia's Prime Minister Vladimir Putin visited the Zhukovsky flight test centre to see the new T-50 fighter. A few months earlier he said that the first pre-series fighters would be delivered to the Air Force's crew conversion centre at Lipetsk in 2013, and by 2015, full-scale production would be launched. (Kremlin.ru)

The Russian State Armament Programme for 2011–2020 (GPV-2020) stipulated the acquisition of 52 PAK FA fighters by 2020. For the following years 2021–2025, the production of 150–160 aircraft was initially planned (which results from the production plans of the UMPO plant in Ufa, producing engines for the Su-57, published at that time). In total, more than 200 fighters were expected to be in service by 2025.

Spare concept of Yuri Borisov

The technical obstacles encountered in the implementation of the Su-57 programme, the unclear position of India and its subsequent withdrawal from the project, Western sanctions after Russia annexed Crimea in 2014 and finally the collapse of oil prices in the same 2014, all caused delays and led to a reduction in the number of aircraft ordered.

The new economical concept was first announced on 23 March 2015, during a visit to the Komsomolsk-on-Amur plant, by the Russian Deputy Defence Minister Yuri Borisov. He said that the MoD would buy fewer fifth-generation T-50 fighters than previously planned in the GPV-2020 programme, taking an increased number of the cheaper Su-30SM and Su-35 fighters instead. The next day, the *Kommersant* daily newspaper, referring to its own source in the MoD, specified that the military would order only one squadron with 12 fighters by 2020, instead of the planned 52 (eight in each year 2016, 2017 and 2018, and 14 in each year 2019 and 2020).

Yuri Borisov specially praised the Su-35S, saying that its capabilities approached the PAK FA, except for the stealth features. Later in July 2018, Borisov, the then already Deputy Prime Minister of the Russian government, told Russian television that, 'Su-35 is considered one of the best airplanes in the world and therefore we have no reason today to force mass production of the fifth-generation aircraft'. The Su-35 'is not inferior even to the first-stage Su-57', he said. It is not known if this was a compliment; Borisov's words can be read both ways: if the Su-35 is not inferior to the Su-57, it means that the Su-57 is not better than the Su-35. According to Borisov's concept, the Su-57 was to be kept 'in reserve' and large-scale production was to be launched further into the future, when it was realised that the Su-30 and Su-35 were inferior to their rivals. Meanwhile, the Su-57 is much more expensive than the current production fighters.

The promise to buy 12 Su-57 fighters by 2020 also turned out to be too optimistic. There was silence for several years until the beginning of 2018 when Yuri Borisov announced on Russian television that the MoD 'intends to conclude soon a contract for a batch of Su-57s for test-combat operation, with the delivery in 2019'. On 22 August 2018, at the Army 2018 exhibition, implementing this frugal concept, Russia's Deputy Defence Minister for Acquisitions Aleksey Krivoruchko and the UAC President Yuri Slyusar inked a contract for two Su-57 fighters to be delivered to Russia's Aerospace Forces, one in 2019 and one in 2020. During the signing ceremony Krivoruchko said that within the following several years, the service 'intends to receive fifteen production Su-57s'.

A breakthrough on Putin's orders: three Su-57 regiments by 2028

A radical turn in the Su-57 programme occurred on 15 May 2019, when at a conference in Sochi with military and industry authorities, Russia's President Vladimir Putin announced a purchase of 76 Su-57 fighters. 'We need to fully re-equip three Aerospace Force air regiments with the Su-57 fifth-generation advanced air system by 2028', he said, and continued: 'I hope... that a contract for the comprehensive supply of 76 fighters with modern weapons and modernised ground infrastructure will be concluded in the near future.' A formal order was placed by Russia's MoD at Sukhoi a month later, on 27 June, during the Army 2019 exhibition in Kubinka, outside Moscow.

Seventy-six fighters are sufficient for three regiments of a reduced complement, with two 12-ship squadrons each; the full complement of a tactical aviation regiment in Russia comprises three squadrons. The remaining four aircraft will probably be assigned to the 4th Crew Conversion Centre at Lipetsk.

Vladimir Putin said in Sochi that the current state armament programme for 2018–2027 (GPV-2027) had provided for the purchase of only 16 Su-57 fighters. However, after the negotiations, Putin continued, 'the involved companies reduced the cost of the aircraft and arms by almost 20 per cent', which enabled the increase of the order to 76 aircraft 'without an increase in costs', however weird it sounds. It probably means that the Su-57 price was reduced so much that it is possible to purchase 76 of these fighters for the price envisaged previously for 16 Su-57s and a larger number of Su-35S fighters. Both types are manufactured by the same production facility in Komsomolsk-on-Amur.

The order for a large batch of Su-57 fighters will certainly help to perfect this new platform, which cannot be done with the prototypes or low-rate initial production aircraft only.

Before the conference in Sochi, on 14 May 2018, Vladimir Putin visited the 929 GLITs test centre in Akhtubinsk, where the Su-57 state trials were being conducted. Six Su-57 fighters joined him when the presidential Il-96-300 RA-96022 was approaching the airfield. Putin later met with the pilots who accompanied him in the air, asking for an opinion on the Su-57. The answers were vague, along the lines of, 'the trials are still going on' and 'not everything is checked and assessed yet'. General Radik Bariyev, the head of the 929 GLITs, told Russian television that the Su-57 still requires 'a wide range of trials, which we are now dealing with. The first is reduced visibility; we already have good results here... I would not like

Above and right: Vladimir Putin arriving at Akhtubinsk test centre in May 2018 on his Il-96-300 assisted by six Su-57 fighters. (Kremlin.ru)

to give specific characteristics yet, but this airplane will be the best in the world, believe me'. Another pilot added: 'This is a good leap into the future'. Of note, is that when asked by Putin about his salary, a military test pilot with the rank of colonel replied that he was earning 140,000 roubles (around £1,500) per month, to which others immediately responded that they earned less.

The launch of serial production of the Su-57

The Su-57 trials were still ongoing and their condition did not allow for series production of the fighter. However, understanding the importance of this aircraft for the future of the Russian Aerospace Forces and the aviation industry, on 3 May 2017, the then Deputy Minister of Defence Yuri Borisov signed the ordinance: 'On the commencement of preparations for serial production of the T-50 before the completion of the development work.' The serial aircraft configuration was approved back in April 2016; it corresponds to the last of the test aircraft, the T-50-11.

After receiving an order in August 2018 for two Su-57 fighters of the initial series, with the internal designation T-50S, the KnAAZ plant in Komsomolsk-on-Amur began their construction. On 8 November 2019, Deputy Defence Minister Alexei Krivoruchko visited the KnAAZ plant, where he got acquainted with the production status of the first Su-57. The Zvezda television channel of the

The first initial-series Su-57, T-50S-1, under assembly at KnAAZ. The aircraft was to be the first Su-57 delivered to the Russian Air Force, but it crashed on 24 December 2019, before the delivery. (Archives)

MoD showed in the production hall the almost ready first serial T-50S-1 aircraft with a blue tactical number '01'. The aircraft was already painted with a dark grey pixel camouflage similar to the last T-50 prototypes. A plaque with the serial number of the fighter, 51001, was installed on the scaffolding. Krivoruchko said in Komsomolsk: 'The aircraft will be delivered to the Aerospace Forces by the end of the year. We are expecting another such aircraft next year, and then production will increase many times over.' The second serial Su-57 was also shown in the television report; it was at a much less advanced stage of production.

Information about the delivery of the first serial new generation Su-57 fighter was to be a key point of a meeting of the MoD leadership with Vladimir Putin, which took place on 24 December 2019. However, a few hours before the conference, the Su-57 '01' crashed. It was the first aircraft of its type that was lost. Before, the most serious incident was the failure on 10 June 2014 when the fifth prototype, T-50-5, caught fire on the runway after landing at Zhukovsky; it resumed flight tests after 16 months of reconstruction.

The aircraft crashed on 24 December 2019 at 11:14 local time, 120km from the airfield in Komsomolsk-on-Amur, during a handover flight before its scheduled delivery a few days later; reportedly, it was the fourth flight of this aircraft. The pilot, Alexei Gorshkov from the 485th Military Mission of the MoD at the Komsomolsk-on-Amur factory ejected himself successfully. Of note, eight years earlier, on 28 February 2012, Gorshkov was a co-pilot of Lieutenant Colonel Valery Kirilin, with whom he crashed near the same place on an Su-30MK2 fighter; the crew ejected successfully then also.

At the moment of the crash, the aircraft formally still belonged to the manufacturer, the UAC, so the accident was being dealt with by civil authorities. The causes of the accident were investigated by a commission headed by the Deputy Minister of Industry Oleg Bocharov. According to the accident report, 'the accident with Su-57 aircraft occurred due to a combination of two factors: incorrect adjustment of the first channel of BUP-50 [drive control unit] of the left tailplane section as a result of violation of requirements of operating manual of the KSU-50-01 [flight control system], and a failure of processor "A" of the BU-7 module of the ShS-80-01 block of the KSU-50-01 system.' In short, the manufacturer incorrectly adjusted the tailplane drive, and this overlapped with a failure of one of the processors of the flight control system.

Above and right: The second initial-series Su-57, T-50S-2, in the final assembly hall of the KnAAZ plant in August 2020. The aircraft did not have one of the engines, some covers were not yet installed and the radar nose cone was temporary. Later, it performed its first flight on 31 October 2020. (UAC)

On 12 August 2020, the KnAAZ plant was visited by Russia's Defence Minister Sergei Shoygu, accompanied by Deputy Minister Alexei Krivoruchko. In the hall they visited, the assembly of the second Su-57 of the preliminary series, '51002' or T-50S-2, was being completed. The T-50S-2 took off for the first time on 31 October 2020. After the T-50S-1 crashed, the T-50S-2 then became the first Su-57 handed over to the Russian Aerospace Forces.

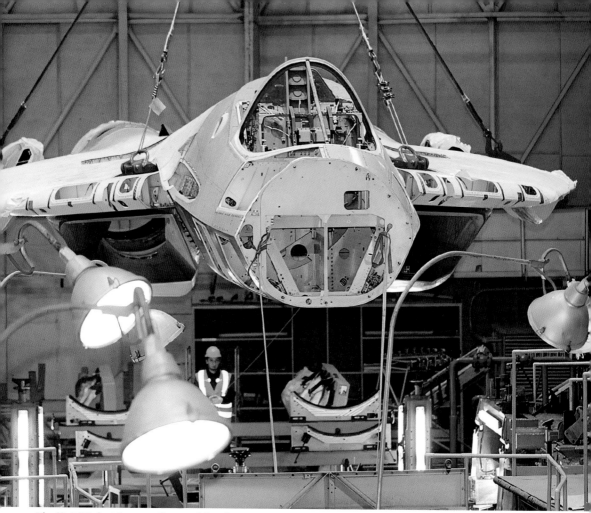

The KnAAZ plant is currently organising the Su-57 production line. An important task set by the MoD is to reduce the cost of aircraft production. (KnAAZ)

The Su-57 '01', or T-50S-2, was the first aircraft to be formally handed over to the Russian Ministry of Defence in December 2020. Here, the fighter's airframe is being covered with a special radar-absorbing paint before delivery. (Archives)

The long-awaited event, the handover of the first new Su-57 fighter for service in the Russian Aerospace Forces, took place in December 2020. On 24 December 2020, the Su-57 '01blue' took off from the airfield of the Sukhoi Komsomolsk-on-Amur Aviation Plant (KnAAZ) and headed west. The first stop was in Ulan-Ude, 1,240nm (2,300km) west of Komsomolsk, where the aircraft had to stay until the next day because of bad weather conditions. The next day, the aircraft arrived in Novosibirsk, 810nm (1,500km) from Ulan-Ude, for refueling and continued its flight to Akhtubinsk, another 1,400nm (2,600km) to the west, the site of the MoD's 929th State Flight Test Centre.

The plan for 2021 envisages the delivery of four Su-57s, which will be deployed to the 4th State Air Personnel Preparation and Military Evaluation Centre at Lipetsk, 190nm (350km) south of Moscow. The task of the centre is to train instructors from operational units that are to receive the new type of aircraft; these instructors will then train pilots in their regiments. The centre is also to develop tactics for the combat use of the new aircraft and to write appropriate manuals for pilots.

The first batch of Su-57 fighters will not go to an operational unit until 2022. On 21 December 2020, in his speech at a meeting of the Collegium of the Ministry of Defence, the minister Sergei Shoygu declared that, within the contract of 2019 for 76 Su-57 aircraft, the Aerospace Forces will receive 22 fighters by 2024. A fighter aviation regiment in Russia has 24 aircraft, which means that only in 2025 will the first Su-57 operational unit be fully completed. Deliveries will speed up later, and in 2028, Russia is to have three Su-57 regiments.

Su-57E for export

The Sukhoi design bureau received from its parent structure, Sukhoi holding, a contract for the development of an export version of the new fighter, then designated I-21E, on 14 August 2003, three weeks after receiving the contract from the Russian MoD for the I-21 (PAK FA). The general shape of the I-21E was approved on 28 June 2006.

Russia only formally began offering the Su-57E aircraft for export in 2018. Yuri Slyusar claimed in August 2018 that the Su-57 will be 'significantly cheaper' than US F-22 and F-35 fighters, without giving any numbers, however. In early May 2019, on the wave of enthusiasm in Russia after Turkey purchased the S-400 anti-aircraft systems, Sergei Chemezov, the CEO of Rostech, in an interview with the Turkish press, offered the Su-57 to Turkey, more in propaganda than in fact.

During the MAKS 2019 airshow in Zhukovsky, a close-up of the Su-57 was presented for the first time at the static exposition (before Su-57s were shown only in flight). The non-flying T-50-KNS appeared there under the export designation Su-57E and the number '057'. The MAKS 2019 opening ceremony was attended by the President of Turkey Recep Tayyip Erdoğan who was invited by the President of Russia Vladimir Putin. Relations between Russia and Turkey were very warm at the time, even despite the shooting down of the Russian Su-24M by a Turkish F-16C in Syria in November 2015. Turkey recently bought Russian S-400 anti-aircraft missile systems, and now the Russians also wanted to sell combat aircraft to Turkey. It was the subject of talks in Zhukovsky; Putin personally showed Erdoğan the Su-57E. However, judging from various statements by Russian officials, Turkey has actually been offered the Su-35, and the Su-57 is possibly a matter for the much longer-term. In turn, according to statements from the Turkish side, including the Minister of Foreign Affairs, Mevlüt Çavuşoğlu, the purchase by Turkey of the Su-35, and even more so the Su-57, are 'at a very preliminary stage', which is a diplomatic way of saying that they have not been carried out.

Two countries that have recently purchased significant batches of Russian MiG-29M and Su-35 fighters, and could possibly be interested in the Su-57E, are Algeria and Egypt. In Asia, Vietnam is the most likely customer. The rest of the traditional buyers of Russian military technology either want to build similar aircraft indigenously, as with China and India, or cannot afford such an expensive system, as is the case with the post-Soviet countries.

Above and left: A non-flying T-50-KNS (Kompleksnyi Naturnyi Stend (complex full-scale stand)) mock-up presented as an Su-57E export version at the MAKS 2019 static exposition. (Piotr Butowski)

Vladimir Putin presents Su-57E to the President of Turkey, Recep Tayyip Erdoğan, during the MAKS 2019 opening ceremony. (Aviasalon)

Chapter 8
Su-57 in Detail

Mikhail Strelets, director of Sukhoi design bureau and current head of the Su-57 programme, in material published in March 2020 by UAC, shared some interesting information about the goals that were set for making the Su-57. Most of them are typical for the fifth-generation fighter. Strelets mentioned stealth operations, including low radar cross-section, supersonic cruising speed and supersonic manoeuvrability. He particularly emphasised the 'high level of automation and high intellectualisation of combat operations, and interoperability with automated command systems'. The Su-57's fire-control system 'has the ability to omnidirectional and multi-channel use of the weapons'.

However, in the first place Mikhail Strelets stated that from the very beginning, the Su-57 was designed as a multi-role aircraft, combining the functions of a fighter and strike aircraft. As Russians decided on only one type of new fighter, they could not divide the missions between a heavy fighter, optimised for air superiority, and a lightweight one, optimised for strike missions. Therefore, in first place among the requirements for the Su-57 is a multifunction capability: fighting all kinds of tactical targets, aerial, ground and surface, situated in any position. It will be accomplished thanks to a multitude of sensors providing the pilot with full orientation in the situation around the aircraft, as well as a wide range of guided munitions. The aircraft received very roomy internal weapon bays. Strelets emphasised this as the most important difference between the Su-57 and the US fifth-generation aircraft, the F-22 and F-35.

'The F-22 was originally created as an air-superiority aircraft. But only then did the Americans, realizing that it was fundamentally wrong to design an aircraft only for deploying air-to-air missiles, made an attempt to fit air-to-surface weapons in the existing configuration of the bays. But the geometry of the compartments did not allow accommodating larger loads.' In turn, 'the characteristics of the F-35 as a fighter – acceleration and manoeuvrability – are inferior even to fourth-generation aircraft, not to mention the Su-57', Mikhail Strelets summarised.

As a distinguishing feature of the Su-57 among other new fighters, Mikhail Strelets also mentioned its super manoeuvrability, that is, reaching angles of attack of 60–70° while maintaining controllability, and the ability to reach 100° for a while without losing stability. 'In the West... they focus more on beyond-visual range combat than on close-air combat. We focus on both, to make our aircraft superior both in close and in long-range combat.' Strelets also said that the Su-57 can land on short runways and its landing length is 'about two times less than that of the best fourth-generation aircraft, Su-35'.

Similarly, the Sukhoi company in its official publications, lists the most important characteristics of the Su-57 as follows:

- multifunction capability – the ability to combat air, ground and sea surface targets at day and night, and in any weather;
- high manoeuvrability and flight performance;
- continuous supersonic cruising flight;
- short take-off and landing;
- low radar and infrared visibility;
- omnidirectional and multi-channel use of weapons against both air and ground (including sea) targets;
- high level of aircraft protection by passive and active countermeasures;
- high interference immunity of sensors and weapons.

Aerodynamic configuration

The Su-57 can perform supersonic cruise flight without afterburner and, most importantly, it can manoeuvre and fight at that speed. It imposes high requirements for the aircraft's aerodynamic layout, engines (high thrust without afterburner) and mission systems (quick reaction). The aerodynamic configuration of the Su-57 is aimed at achieving a high lift-to-drag ratio at supersonic speed, much higher than in the previous generation fighters, which enables performing supersonic cruise flight without afterburner; the aircraft maintains a high lift-to-drag ratio at subsonic speed at the same time.

The aircraft features a blended-body configuration with a lift-generating fuselage. The wing outer sections are trapezoidal in shape, with a high-sweep angle at the leading edge, a long chord at the root and a short chord at the tip. This configuration enables a wing to be thick at the root but still have a low relative thickness, which reduces drag at near and supersonic airspeeds.

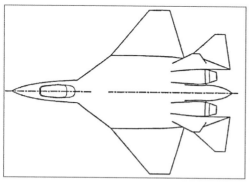

Sukhoi has applied twice for a patent of 'The aircraft of integral aerodynamic configuration' (the name 'T-50' was not included, of course). For the first time in 2009, when no one has seen the aircraft yet (see first image). The second time – in January 2012, that is after the first flight of the T-50, when its external shape was already known (see second image). The old children's game of 'find ten differences' is reduced to just one here. The first patent does not show the most interesting and long secret element of the fighter's aerodynamic configuration: the moving leading-edge flaps at the fuselage side extensions. (Sukhoi)

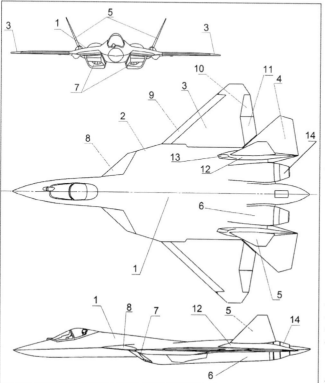

Aerodynamic configuration of the Su-57:
1 – fuselage
2 – fuselage side extension
3 – wing outer panel
4 – all-moving tailplanes
5 – all-moving tailfins
6 – engine nacelles
7 – engine air intakes
8 – moving leading-edge flap at the fuselage side extension
9 – nose flap
10 – aileron
11 – flaperon
12 – tailfin pylon
13 – air intakes for engine compartments' cooling and for heat exchangers of the air conditioning system
14 – vectored-thrust engine nozzle

Above left: The T-50's aerodynamic layout features strongly forward-stretched fuselage side extensions ended by large moving flaps on the leading edge, connected with the fuselage by elastic couplings. (UAC)

Above right: Su-57 is a statically unstable aircraft at supersonic speed and can manoeuvre at that speed much better than any previous fighter. (UAC)

The most characteristic feature of the T-50's aerodynamic layout is the strongly forward-stretched fuselage side extensions ended by large moving flaps on the leading edge, connected with the fuselage by elastic couplings. These extensions shift the centre of pressure forward, increasing the static instability of the aircraft (the greater it is the more manoeuvrable is the aircraft). This is especially important in supersonic flight, where the centre of pressure naturally shifts rearward and the aircraft becomes excessively stable and less manoeuvrable. Thanks to high static instability, the Su-57 can manoeuvre at a supersonic speed much better than any previous fighter. In cruising flight, the movable front fuselage flaps perform a function similar to the wing nose flaps, i.e. the flaps increase lift force. When flying at beyond-stalling angles of attack (up to about 90°), its downward deflection increases the diving torque and thus enables the aircraft to return to level flight in the event of the failure of the movable engine nozzles.

The wing high-lift devices comprise nose flaps, ailerons and flaperons. The nose flaps are used to increase the critical angle of attack and ensure smooth flow around the wing during take-off, landing, manoeuvring and in cruising flight at subsonic speed. Ailerons and flaperons are designed for roll control when deflected differentially; flaperons additionally increase lift during take-off and landing when deflected down.

The empennage, both horizontal and vertical, is all-moving and can be deflected together or differentially. The tailplanes provide the ability to control the aircraft in the longitudinal channel, when deflected together, and in the lateral channel when deflected differentially, at near and supersonic flight speeds. They are installed on the fuselage side tail booms; this enables an increase in the distance between the supports, which, in turn, reduces the loads on the airframe and, accordingly, reduces weight. In addition, the pylons cover hydraulic drives of the horizontal and vertical empennage, which, due to the removal of the hydraulic drives outside the fuselage, enables an increase in the volume of the weapon bays between the engine nacelles.

The all-moving vertical fins provide the aircraft's stability and controllability at all flight speeds when deflected together; when rotated differentially, they act as an air brake. The vertical empennage is mounted on pylons located on the fuselage side tail booms; in the front part of the pylons there are air intakes for the engine compartments' cooling and for heat exchangers of the air conditioning system.

Another control element is the moving engine nozzles. The engines are housed in wide-spaced nacelles; this enables a large weapon compartment to be placed between them. To counter the turning moment in case of the failure of one of the engines, their axes are yawed to the sides, so that the thrust

Above: Su-57's control surfaces include large front fuselage flaps, wing nose flaps, ailerons and flaperons, all-moving tailfins and tailplanes, as well as vectored-thrust engine nozzles. (Piotr Butowski)

Left: During MAKS 2019, Su-57 demonstrated a very short run (estimated below 200m) thanks to the release of the braking parachute before it touched the ground. (Piotr Butowski)

Below: Su-57 deploys thrust vectoring to shorten its landing run. (Piotr Butowski)

Above left: One of initial models of Su-57 tested by TsAGI, the MMS-112T, used to develop the fighter's wing high lift devices and control surfaces. (Piotr Butowski)

Above right: Twenty-eight various models of the future Su-57 were examined in TsAGI's wind tunnels. (TsAGI)

vector of the operating engine passes closer to the centre of mass of the aircraft. The engines are fitted with moving axisymmetric nozzles that can be deflected together or differentially. The deflection is carried out in planes inclined at an acute angle to the plane of symmetry of the aircraft and enables control of the aircraft in all channels.

The aircraft is controlled by a KSU-50-01 (Kompleksnaya Sistema Upravleniya (complex control system)) developed by Moscow-based MNPK Avionika company; early prototypes have the initial KSU-50 version of the system.

The Central Aerohydrodynamic Institute (TsAGI) based at Zhukovsky outside Moscow, does not construct aircraft. Its task is to conduct advanced research and present the ideas to design bureaus for implementation. Before a new aircraft is built, various variants of its aerodynamic configuration undergo many hours of testing at TsAGI's wind tunnels.

Starting in 1999, specialists of the institute conducted unique settlement researches of configuration of the future Su-57. In the TsAGI wind tunnels, 28 various models of the aircraft were investigated; the total number of tests exceeded 32,000. Together with the staff of the Sukhoi design bureau, TsAGI scientists have developed the aerodynamic shape of the Su-57 and the KSU-50 flight control system for a manoeuvrable aircraft that is statically unstable in the lateral and longitudinal control channels. A unique adjustable, low-visible air intake was created, which ensures stable engine operation in all flight modes. TsAGI carried out work to ensure safety from a flutter. Ensuring the strength of the airframe structure with the widespread use of new materials was another task that TsAGI scientists have successfully solved. Tests of new materials and structural elements have been successfully completed.

After the start of flight testing of the T-50 prototype aircraft, the research continues: the aerodynamic characteristics of the aircraft are clarified, compared with the results of flight tests, and the safety of releasing of new weapon types from the aircraft's weapon bays is worked out.

Stealth features

In December 2013, Sukhoi published a patent for *Multifunctional aircraft with a reduced radar signature*, from which one can learn about the low-visibility technology solutions implemented in the Su-57 fighter. The patent specification states that the Su-27 fighter has an effective radar cross-section of $10–15m^2$,

Su-57 on a rotating platform for testing stealth characteristics of various objects at the Air Force Academy in Voronezh. The platform has a load capacity of 100 tonnes, and the entire complex is called Yegorevets. (Russia's MoD)

while the purpose of implementing the patent presented is 'to reduce radar section to an average figure of $0.1-1.0$ m². According to the patent, 'the effective radar cross section is determined by three factors:

- airframe shape... including air intake and air duct;
- the structure of the airframe elements... the covering and hatches contacts, and the contacts between the moving and fixed parts of the airframe;
- the use of radar absorbing materials and coatings.'

According to the patent, the main solution to reduce the radar visibility is the internal weapons' carriage. The inlet guides for engine compressors generate 'a significant portion (up to 60%) of the effective radar cross section of the airframe-power plant system in the front hemisphere'. That is why, radar blockers reducing reflections from the engine inlet guide vanes are installed inside the engine air ducts.

The shape of the airframe has been selected to reduce the number of directions of reflection of the electromagnetic waves and because these directions are possibly the safest. The angles of sweep of the front fuselage flaps, wing and tailplane leading and trailing edges, edges of the air intakes and hatch covers have been reduced to three figures, deflected from the aircraft's axis. Similarly, in the cross-section, the fuselage sides, lateral edges of the air intakes and vertical empennage are deflected at the same angle. Some openings and slots on the airframe's surface, for example, the boundary-layer bleeds on the sides of the air intakes and openings on the upper fuselage, immediately aft of the cockpit are covered with a thick grid with the mesh smaller than ¼ of the wavelength of the 'attacking' radar, which reduces reflections from these uneven surfaces. Gaps between the airframe elements are filled with conducting sealants, which also reduces the radar cross-section. The glazing of the cockpit canopy is metallised. Radar-absorbing and shielding materials and coatings are used.

Another group of undertakings concerns the fighter's equipment. The surfaces of the N036 radar arrays are deflected from the vertical plane, thus deflecting the enemy radar's radiation aside. The domes of the arrays are selective – they let through their own signal and block other frequencies. Additionally, the edges of the array compartments have curtains covered with a radar-absorbing coating to avoid the effect caused by a freak wave, when a wave multiple is reflected in an enclosed space and radar returns outside are amplified. In order to reduce the total number of arrays, the available arrays are used by multiple systems simultaneously, for example, the radar and electronic countermeasures (ECM) systems. In the antenna-feeder system, antennas not protruding outside the airframe outlines are used, and the vertical empennage serves as a communications suite antenna. The turret of the 101KS-V sight is rotated backwards in the cruise position, and its rear hemisphere is covered with a radar-absorbing coating.

Power plant

Su-57 is powered by two AL-41F1 (izdeliye 117) thrust-vectoring turbofan engines, each rated at 14.5 tonnes with afterburner and approximately 9 tonnes of dry thrust. Sukhoi ordered this engine from the Lyulka-Saturn design bureau in April 2004. According to the contract, the AL-41F-1 engine was to have a fuel consumption of 0.655kg/kGh.

The AL-41F-1 engine is a thorough upgrade of the AL-31F from the Su-27/Su-30 with a larger diameter fan, new high- and low-pressure turbines, an upgraded combustion chamber and new full authority digital engine control system, integrated with the aircraft's control system. A version of this engine with a different control unit, the AL-41F-1S (117S) powers the Su-35 fighter. The AL-41F-1S engine began flight tests in March 2004 on an experimental Su-27M '710' fighter, first with one new engine, and from June 2005 – with two.

Trials of the AL-41F-1 engine for the Su-57 began on 21 January 2010, only a week before the first flight of the T-50, on the same experimental '710' aircraft. On 17 April 2018, the certificate of completing the AL-41F-1 engine's state bench trials run by the 4th Research Department of the 929 GLITs at Chkalovsky was formally signed.

The VSU-117 auxiliary power unit on the Su-57 ensures a high autonomy of deployment, reduction in fuel consumption during ground preparations and an economy of the life of the main engines.

In addition to fuel inside the airframe, the Su-57 can take additional fuel tanks. Conventional underwing tanks come in two sizes: PTB-2000 and PTB-3400 for 2,000 and 3,400 litres, respectively (PTB stands for 'podvesnoi toplivnyi bak' (suspended fuel tank)). In addition, the Su-57 can also take additional fuel in the internal weapons chambers; VTB-M and VTB-B plug-in tanks are used for this (VTB stands for 'vkladnoi toplivnyi bak' (plug-in fuel tank), and the letters M and B mean 'malyi' (small) and 'bolshoi' (big)). All additional fuel tanks for the Su-57 are produced by the Sukhoi plant in Novosibirsk.

Lyulka AL-41F-1S (izdeliye 117S) turbofan engine for the Su-35S fighter; the Su-57 is powered by the insignificantly different AL-41F-1 version with the same thrust of 14.5 tonnes with afterburner. (Piotr Butowski)

Left: Two widely spaced AL-41F-1 turbofan engines give the impression that the entire structure of the Su-57 is attached to them. The fuselage between the engines is occupied by two massive weapons bays. (Piotr Butowski)

Below: Su-57 and Su-35S replenish fuel from a Il-78 tanker. The first test of the in-flight refuelling was made by the T-50-2 prototype in August 2012. (Russia's MoD)

Below left and below right: T-50-9 prototype carries two PTB-3400 drop fuel tanks. In addition, Su-57 can also take additional fuel in the internal weapon compartments. (Sukhoi)

Sukhoi Su-57 Specifications (estimated)

Wingspan	14.1m (46ft 3in)
Length	20.1m (66ft)
Height	4.6m (15ft 1in)
Empty weight	18,000kg (39,683lb)
Nominal take-off weight	25,000kg (55,116lb)
Maximum take-off weight	35,000kg (77,162lb)
Maximum speed	Mach 2.0
Supersonic cruising speed	Mach 1.3
Maximum supersonic range	810 nautical miles (1,500km)
Maximum range	1,890 nautical miles (3,500km)

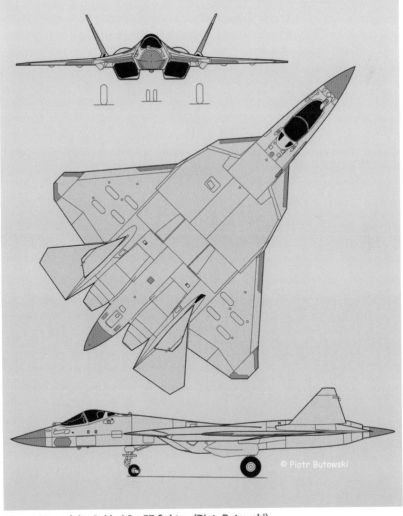

Three views of the Sukhoi Su-57 fighter. (Piotr Butowski)

Sensors fusion

Sensor fusion is a standard requirement for a fifth-generation fighter, and all the Su-57's systems and sensors are coupled and controlled by an IUS (Informatsionno-upravlayushchaya Sistema) information and control system. The Sukhoi design bureau is responsible for the IUS, which is a novelty. In the past, fire-control and flight navigation systems were integrated by instrument companies; on Sukhoi fighters, this work was usually entrusted to RPKB of Ramenskoye. The computer system for IUS has been developed by GRPZ from Ryazan.

The IUS is responsible for the interaction between the pilot and the on-board equipment systems. Due to new functions of the avionics, the pilot's workload has increased dramatically, so much attention has been paid to its reduction. The IUS has implemented 'intellectual support' for the pilot; it consists of the maximum automation of the process of target searching, aiming the aircraft at the target, and preparing the weapon for use. At the same time, in the background, the task of ensuring the aircraft's self-defence is being solved.

The fully 'glass' cockpit has no analogue indicators. All the necessary information is displayed on two large, connected side-by-side, MFI-50 multifunction displays by RPKB, as well as a head-up display ShKAI-50 by Elektroavtomatika of St Petersburg. In the final version of the cockpit, two connected MFI-50 displays will be replaced by one widescreen display with folded sides. In the cockpit there is also a small multifunction MFPI-50 display and control panel by RPKB.

In close air combat, the target indication is provided using the NSTsI-50 helmet-mounted sight and display by Elektroavtomatika. For better information support for the pilot, there is a voice warning system. When displaying information on indicators, the principle 'the right information at the right moment' is implemented; information from various sources is integrated. Controls for all major functions are located on the aircraft and engine control sticks (HOTAS).

The Su-57's single pilot is provided with a K-36D-5 ejection seat, as well as the SOZhE-50 (Sistema Obespecheniya Zhiznedeyatelnosti Ekipazha) crew life-support system, that includes a KS-50 oxygen installation with BKDU-50 generator, anti-g installation, anti-g PPK-7 or high-altitude VKK-17 flight suit, KM-36M oxygen mask and ZSh-10NB helmet, all developed by the Zvezda Company in Tomilino. The use of an on-board oxygen generator BKDU-50 (instead of an oxygen cylinder) provides virtually unlimited flight time and no need for ground oxygen refuelling.

The K36D-5 seat has, compared with the current K36D-3.5 used on other Russian fighters, better minimum allowable altitudes and speeds of ejection as well as an extended range of permissible pilot weight. The seat ensures safe ejection of the pilot in the altitude range from 0 to 20km and instrument speeds from 0 to 1,300km/h, including the zero-zero range. The weight of the pilot with kit can be from 55kg to 125kg.

The ZSh-10NB (Zashchitnyi Shlem) helmet is adapted to fitting an NSTsI-50 helmet-mounted sight and display; the helmet is available in two sizes.

Typical Su-57 pilot's outfit on the fifth-generation K-36D-5 ejection seat. The installation behind it is the KS-50 oxygen system. (Piotr Butowski)

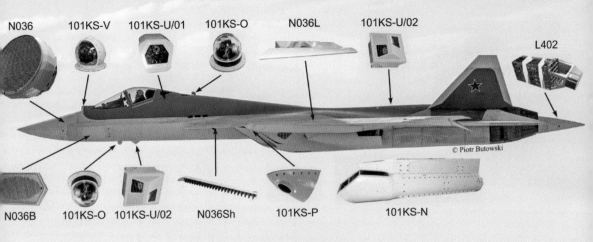

N036　101KS-V　101KS-U/01　101KS-O　N036L　101KS-U/02

L402

© Piotr Butowski

N036B　101KS-O　101KS-U/02　N036Sh　101KS-P　101KS-N

Above: Su-57's radar and electro-optical sensors provide all-round surveillance, targeting and self-protection. (Piotr Butowski)

Right: The Su-57's cockpit features two large MFI-50 displays, a small MFPI-50 display and control panel, and a ShKAI-50 head-up display. (Russia's MoD)

Wide-angle ShKAI-50 head-up display by the Elektroavtomatika company. (Piotr Butowski)

Sh121 radar suite

Su-57's fire-control systems include the MIRES (Sh121) radio-electronic suite and OEIS (101KS) electro-optical suite; both of these systems also perform aircraft self-defence tasks.

In 2003, the Zhukovsky-based Tikhomirov NIIP institute won the competition for the MIRES (Mnogofunktsyonalnaya Integrirovannaya Radio-Elektronnaya Sistema (multifunction integrated radio-electronic system)) for the fifth-generation fighter. The MIRES or Sh121 suite consists of the N036 radar system by NIIP, the N036Sh identification friend or foe (IFF) by GRPZ, and the L402 ECM system by KNIRTI.

The chief designer of the N036 radar at NIIP is Vladimir Zagorodny; the chief designer of the antennas is Anatoly Sinani. A large part of the Sh121 system design work was carried out by Ryazan-based GRPZ, including the hardware for the N036YeVS computing system, the N036Sh IFF system and the Solo-21 computers used in various parts of the system. The Leninets company from St Petersburg develops software for the N036 radar's automatic low-altitude flight mode, high-resolution mode of the radar, and ensures the electromagnetic compatibility of the electronic equipment (K131-50 system).

The N036 Byelka (squirrel; in fact, it is the codename of the R&D work, which then came to be the name of the radar) has five active electronically scanned arrays (AESA), that together control the air space within the angle up to 270° (+/-135° from the aircraft's axis). The whole N036 radar is controlled by the N036YeVS (Yedinaya Vychislitelnaya Sistema) joint computing system made of two Solo-21.01 (initial signal processing) and Solo-21.02 (data processing and radar control) computers, developed and manufactured by GRPZ. The GRPZ plant at Ryazan is also serially producing the N036 radar, including the transceiver modules made from elements supplied by NPP Istok of Fryazino (the X-band) and Guskov Research Institute of Microdevices (then, NII Component institute) of Zelenograd (the L-band). The X-band modules are made on the basis gallium arsenide (GaAs), and the L-band modules are made on the basis of silicon.

The N036-1-01 forward-looking X-band (3cm wavelength) antenna is an oval 84cm (33in) long and 73cm (29in) wide. The array's sheet is made of horizontal stripes containing from 12 to 44 transceiver modules; there are 1,514 modules in total (earlier, at the MAKS 2009 and 2011 exhibitions, an experimental variant of the antenna was presented with a slightly different configuration of the array and 1,526 modules). The array's reflector is tilted upwards by around 15°, because for a mid-altitude fighter most of the targets are above it. The array's angles of view are about +/-60°.

 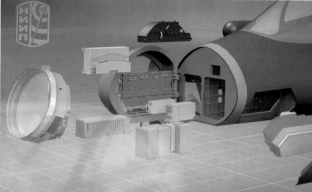

Above left: The N036-1-01 forward-looking X-band (3cm wavelength) antenna is an oval 84cm (33in) long and 73cm (29in) wide, made of 1,514 transceiver modules. The array's reflector is tilted upwards by around 15°. (Piotr Butowski)

Above right: The X-band section of the N036 radar includes a front N036-1-01 aerial and two side N036B-1-01 aerials used for widening the angle of search and tracking targets in azimuth up to +/-135° from the aircraft's axis. (NIIP)

Two smaller N036B-1-01 side-looking X-band arrays consist of 404 transceiver modules each (an early test array shown in 2013 had 358 modules); the array width is about 50cm (20in). The side antennas use similar modules as the front antenna. These smaller arrays are mounted under the forward section of the cockpit, on the lower fuselage sides, and are angled downwards by about 15°. The lateral arrays are used for widening the angle of search and tracking aerial targets in azimuth up to +/-135° from the aircraft's axis, as well as for ground targets. The side antennas have horizontal polarisation, unlike the vertical polarisation of the front antenna. In 2013, NIIP showed the N036B-1-01 side antenna in public for the first time.

Two other N036L-1-01 L-band (decametre wavelength) arrays are mounted in the wing leading edges. Use of L-band radar in air-to-air mode is the Su-57's main means of dealing with stealth targets, which may be detected (but not targeted) by radio waves longer than the X-band for which the radar cross-section's reduction is typically optimised. According to the head of NIIP, Yuri Belyi, computer processing of both signals together, the X-band and the L-band, enables a significant increase in the information efficiency of the radar system.

The N036Sh IFF system has been designed as part of the Pokosnik (mower) programme by Ryazan GRPZ and is being manufactured by the same company. The longitudinal AESA antennas of the IFF interrogator are fitted in the leading edges of the moving flaps of the fuselage side extensions. The N036Sh is a variant of the Type 4283MP IFF system used in the Su-35S fighter. In previous Russian radars, the IFF interrogator antenna was built into the main radar antenna. The separate arrangement of the IFF antenna in the Su-57 (as well as in the Su-35) enables the target identification independently of the basic operation of the radar, as well as on the command of other sensors, for example, the electro-optical targeting device.

Another component of the Sh121 suite is the L402 electronic intelligence and ECM suite, developed within Gimalai (Himalaya) R&D work in KNIRTI institute in Zhukov near Kaluga by a group headed by V N Kuznetsov and manufactured in series by the Signal plant in Stavropol. The L402 detects enemy air-defence or fighter radars that are tracking the Su-57, determines their type and threat level and then activates jamming devices. The L402 ECM suite is provided with its own arrays (for example, contained in a large 'sting' between the engine exhaust nozzles), but when working within the range of the same frequencies as used by the radar it utilises the N036 arrays. The suite is controlled by a Solo-21.402 computer. The first L402 Gimalai system was completed and fitted on a T-50 prototype in 2014.

 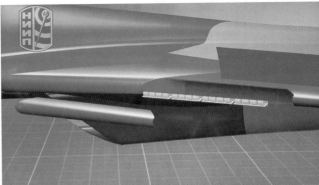

Above left: **NIIP CEO Yuri Belyi (right) and the chief designer of the antenna Anatoly Sinani along with the front AESA antenna of the N036 radar during its first presentation in August 2009. (Piotr Butowski)**

Above right: **The L-band N036L-1-01 aerial is fitted inside the wing front flap. Computer processing of both X and L signals enables a significant increase in the information efficiency of the radar system. (NIIP)**

It was not immediately clear that the radar for PAK FA would have active electronic scanning. Without denying the prospect of using an AESA antenna, NIIP believed that in the first stage, it was necessary to use a passive (PESA) antenna, the technology of which was ready and was much cheaper. NIIP has been making passive electronic scanning radars for many years, including the Zaslon radar for MiG-31, Bars for Su-30MKI and Irbis for Su-35. Incidentally, the Americans have skipped the PESA stage, moving straight from mechanical slot antennas to AESA. Building an active antenna required, first of all, the creation of new small transceiver modules and the launch of their mass and cheap production. However, the Russian Air Force categorically demanded AESA right away, and NIIP was forced to change its position.

Especially for future new radar, the Russians launched, in 2002, anticipatory programmes of mastering new technologies. The GRPZ started the design and production of a new series of Solo computers: first Solo-54 for the N001V radar (Su-27SM), then Solo-35 for the Irbis (Su-35) radar and finally Solo-21 for the Sh121 system (Su-57). The NPP Istok plant in Fryazino near Moscow has mastered the production of microwave monolithic integrated circuits (MMIC) made on the basis of gallium arsenide (GaAs); they operate in the frequency range 8–11GHz and higher, and are used in the construction of X-band transceiver modules. A pilot production line for GaAs MMICs at the NPP Istok plant was launched in 2007. Another NII Component institute in Zelenograd launched a production line of MMICs on the basis of silicon, operating in the L (1–2 GHz) and S (2–4 GHz) bands. The transceiver modules for the Sh121 radar are serially manufactured by the Ryazan GRPZ plant from elements supplied by NPP Istok (X-band) and NPP Pulsar (L-band).

An original requirement for the radar system was all-round coverage in azimuth. The front X-band antenna is fixed and 'looks' at a cone with an aperture angle of +/-60°; two side antennas extend the radar viewing angle to +/-135°. Wide viewing angles give the fighter freedom of manoeuvre; after launching an air-to-air missile with mid-course radio correction or with semi-active radar seeker, the aircraft may turn away from the target without breaking the missile guidance.

NIIP considered a single forward antenna suspended on a movable drive (re-positioner), similar to that of PESA radars Bars and Irbis; a single moving front antenna would be cheaper and require less energy than three antennas. However, according to Yuri Belyi, the cooling of a movable AESA antenna was then technically very difficult, if not impossible. The first project also planned a small rear-facing radar mounted in the fighter's tail, which would provide a truly all-round coverage. However, finding a spot on the aircraft for such a radar was difficult, and eventually the idea was abandoned.

Most of the problems were with the provision of sufficient energy and cooling of the front radar antenna; the antenna weighs 240kg, consumes 11kW of energy and is water-cooled. All of the problems were gradually overcome, and in 2006 the detailed design of the radar was approved. In December 2008, experimental radar with one front antenna was put into operation on a bench. Elements of the new radar were first shown to the public at the MAKS airshow in August 2007; NIIP presented two X-range front antenna stripes, one with 12 and the other with 16 modules, as well as the L-band antenna located in the leading edge of the aircraft wing.

In the spring of 2012, a simplified version of the radar with only the front X-band antenna was installed on the T-50-3 in the Sukhoi workshop in Zhukovsky. It was the third radar made; the previous two underwent laboratory trials. In April 2012, the radar was turned on the ground, and on 26 July, the pilot Sergei Bogdan turned it on for the first time in the air. In 2013, the next two aircraft, the T-50-4 and T-50-5, received radars (still with the front antenna only) already installed at the production plant in Komsomolsk. Soon after, T-50-3 and -4 were equipped with the wing L-band antennas for the first time. Lastly, in 2015, the side-looking X-band antennas were installed on the aircraft. Later, radars were tested in various configurations on other aircraft; additional operating modes of the radar and its interaction with new types of weapons were worked out.

The N036B-1-01 X-band side antenna – it was established on an aeroplane for the first time in 2015. (Piotr Butowski)

ІВНАЯ
ВАННАЯ
РЕШЕТІ
ОБЗОРІ
ЗОНА

The last three of the Su-57 prototypes, T-50-9, -10 and -11, have radars in full completion, with five antennas. The last two aircraft already have radars from the GRPZ serial production plant; the previous radars were produced by the NIIP in co-operation with GRPZ.

101KS electro-optical suite

Another Su-57 fire-control system is the 101KS electro-optical suite, otherwise known as the OEIS (Optiko-Elektronnaya Integrirovannaya Sistema (integrated electro-optical system)), which was developed by Ural Optical-Mechanical Works (UOMZ) of Yekaterinburg, within Atoll R&D work, and produced by the same company. It is intended to provide full control of the space around the aircraft in the optical range, as well as self-defence against missile attack.

The Atoll suite couples a series of sensors, the most prominent of which is the forward 101KS-V (Vozdukh (air)) infrared search and track (IRST) sight in front of the pilot's cockpit. It is an air target detection, recognition and tracking sensor; it can track several air targets simultaneously. Such a sight is typical for all Russian fighter aircraft. The peculiarity of the 101KS-V is that its optical head rotates 180°, and its rear surface is covered with a radar-absorbing layer; in the cruising flight, the turret is turned backwards.

Four ultraviolet missile approach warning sensors (MAWS) cover the whole sphere around the fighter. Two of them, designated 101KS-U/02 (U for ultraviolet), are shaped like a house with two windows, one looking forward and the other to the rear; one such sensor is mounted under the Su-57's forward fuselage and the other on the upper surface of the 'sting' protruding between the engines. Two other 101KS-U/01 side-looking MAWS are mounted on the fuselage sides, just aft of the cockpit.

101KS Atoll electro-optical suite sensors in the front of the Su-57 fuselage.
1. 101KS-V infrared/TV/ laser sight (the sight's eye is rotated backwards here);
2. 101KS-O/N infrared/ laser countermeasures and surveillance turret;
3. side-looking 101KS-U/01 ultraviolet missile-approach warning sensor (MAWS);
4. double-window 101KS-U/02 version of the MAWS, one is looking forward, and the other is looking back; one more 101KS-U/02 is mounted on the upper surface of the rear fuselage. (Piotr Butowski)

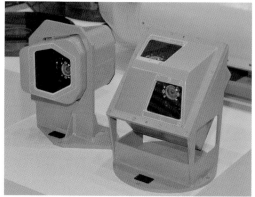

Above left: The 101KS-V infrared search-and-track (IRST) sight enables the target to be seen secretly. The sight's turret is rotated backwards in the cruise position, and its rear surface is covered with a radar-absorbing coating. (Piotr Butowski)

Above right: There are two versions of the ultraviolet missile-approach warning sensors on Su-57. Two single-window 101KS-U/01 sensors are mounted on the fuselage sides. Two double-window 101KS-U/02 sensors are mounted under the Su-57's forward fuselage and on the upper surface of the rear fuselage. (Piotr Butowski)

Left: The 101KS-O/N is declared to be a directional infrared countermeasures (DIRCM) turret used for the fighter's self-defence. Its other purpose is to conduct all-round surveillance in the optical range. (Piotr Butowski)

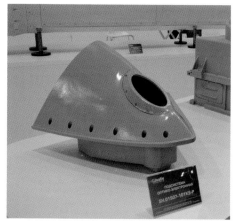

The small 101KS-P imaging infrared sensor supports low-level flying and landing. (Piotr Butowski)

The next two sensors are the 101KS-O/N turrets, one on the fighter's spine and another one under the nose; in this way, both sensors together cover the entire space around the plane. They are declared by UOMZ to be directional infrared countermeasures (DIRCM) used for self-defence of the aircraft. Their other purpose is to conduct all-round surveillance in the optical range.

Another 101KS-P device comprises a small imaging IR sensor to aid low-level flying and landing; it is fitted in the forward section of the left canoe-shaped underwing missile bay. The main task of this sensor is to enable (together with the radar) automatic terrain-following and terrain-avoidance flight at low altitude.

The 101KS-N (nazemnyi (ground)) navigation and targeting pod has been developed for the Su-57. This is a rather conventional device; when developing the 101KS-N, Russia took the American Sniper XR pod as a template. Typically for the class, the pod contains a stabilised platform with TV and 3–5μm thermal imaging cameras (they use a common optical package, including the scanning mirror and automatic tracking unit), a laser rangefinder/target indicator, as well as a laser spot tracker. Factory tests of the first 101KS-N started in 2011.

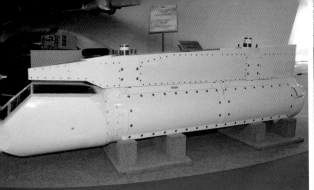

Above left: The 101KS-N navigation and targeting pod that has been developed for the Su-57. (Piotr Butowski)

Above right: 14-round 50mm UV-50-01 decoy dispenser produced by Vympel of Moscow. An interesting fact is that the barrels are covered during the cruise flight. (Piotr Butowski)

The particular selection of the 101KS sensors varied between the T-50 prototypes. Only on the two latest '510' and '511' aircraft has the sensor suite in the configuration intended for the production version of the Su-57 fighter been installed. Early prototypes have only part of the sensors; some have the mock-ups.

The Su-57 has exceptionally extensive self-defence systems. Most of them – ultraviolet 101KS-U warning devices, as well as electronic L402 and infrared 101KS-O countermeasures systems – are already described above. In addition to them, the aircraft has three 14-round 50mm (1.9in) UV-50-01 (Ustroystvo Vybrosa (launching device)) dispensers produced by the Vympel Company of Moscow and intended to launch conventional thermal and radar decoys, as well as single-use programmable ECM transmitters. The dispensers are located in a tail boom between the engine exhaust nozzles. Two launchers shoot sideways upwards, the third one downwards. The essential difference between the UV-50-01 and previous dispensers is the increased variety of cartridge types (eight to ten types). This enables the effective use of a combined set of countermeasures against complex threats, even though the total number of cartridges is limited.

The KPNO-50 flight navigation complex has been developed by RPKB of Ramenskoye. It is built around the BINS-SP-2M inertial navigation by the MIEA institute of Moscow, and controlled by the IVS-50 computing system by RPKB. The Polyot company of Nizhny Novgorod makes the S111-N coded communication system and the AIST-50 antenna-feeder system for the Su-57. The S111-N is used to exchange data with other aircraft as well as ground and airborne command posts. According to the manufacturer, the C111-N has 'much better functional, operational and economic properties than the TKS-2M system' of the Su-27.

Armament

The Su-57 carries its basic ordnance load in two large internal weapon bays that are arranged in tandem, each approximately 0.9m (2ft 11in) wide and 4.4m (14ft 5in) long. The weapon bays occupy the entire length of the fuselage ventral surface, from the nosewheel well to the engine nozzles; each bay can accommodate two missiles or bombs. For internal carriage in these large bays, the Vympel Company developed the UVKU-50 (Unifitsirovannoye Vnutrifyuzelazhnoye Katapultnoye Ustroystvo (unified inside-fuselage ejection device)) ejection release unit. Two models of the launcher are available: the lightweight UVKU-50L for carrying loads up to 300kg (661lb) and the universal UVKU-50U for loads up to 700kg (1,543lb).

Two more missiles are placed inside two so-called 'quick launch' bays in the form of oblong underwing fairings, close to the fuselage; each is for a single small air-to-air missile (AAM) launched from a retractable Vympel VPU-50 (Vnutrifyuzelazhnoye Puskovoye Ustroystvo (inside-fuselage launching device)) rail. The only weapon type that can be carried there is the Vympel R-74M2 (izdeliye 760) close air combat missile.

Above and right: In May 2014, during the Aviamiks show at the Pogonovo training ground near Voronezh, a pair of Su-57s was first shown to the public with Kh-31, R-77 and R-73 missiles suspended under the wings. (Piotr Butowski)

Above left and above right: An Su-57 with a pair of R-77 beyond-visual range air-to-air missiles. (Piotr Butowski)

Left: An Su-57 carries its basic weapon set in two tandem compartments inside the fuselage, and two smaller 'quick-launch' bays under the wing. (Piotr Butowski)

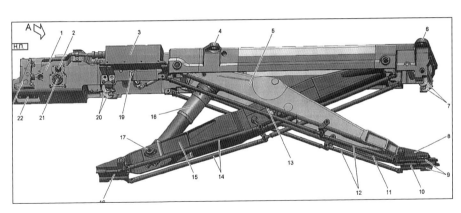

The UVKU-50 ejection weapon release unit is fitted inside the Su-57 fuselage and can carry a missile weighing up to 300kg (L version) or 700kg (U version). (Vympel)

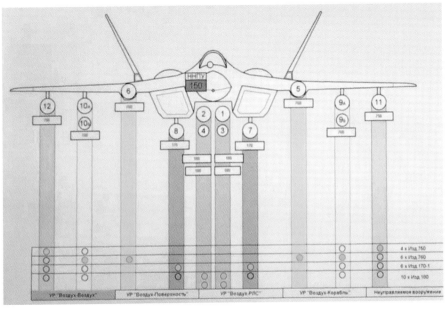

The Su-57 has ten weapon and stores pylons, including four pylons inside two large internal fuselage weapon bays, two pylons inside underwing 'quick launch' bays and six external hardpoints under the wing and the air inlets; the underwing pylons closer to the fuselage may accommodate twin rails. (Russia's MoD)

In missions not requiring stealth, the aircraft may carry a heavier armament load that does not fit in the internal bays, using four pylons under the wing and two under the air inlets. The underwing pylons closer to the fuselage may accommodate twin rails. Weapons use is managed by the RSUO-5 (izdeliye 5PR) store management system.

An NNPU-50 (Nesyomnaya Nepodvizhnaya Pushechnaya Ustanovka (non-detachable unmovable gun mount)) with a GSh-301 (9A1-4071K) 30mm single-barrel cannon and 150 cartridges is located within the starboard wing root.

In May 2014, during the Aviamiks show at the Pogonovo training ground near Voronezh, a pair of Su-57s was first shown to the public with the Kh-31 R-77 and R-73 missiles suspended under the wings. The Tactical Missile Corporation (KTRV) CEO Boris Obnosov said in February 2020 that the developers 'did not have any problems with externally carried weapons. But to fit a missile inside the fuselage, smaller dimensions, folding wings and fins are required. There are also certain difficulties at the missile launch from an enclosed space, as additional loads on the airplane arise.'

Trials of internal-carriage weapons began unexpectedly late. The Su-57 fired a missile from the internal weapon bay for the first time on 16 March 2016; the type of weaponry is unknown. It is of note that this only happened more than six years after the first flight of the T-50 prototype, although this had been promised

Above: A GSh-301 (9A1-4071K) 30mm single-barrel cannon of the Su-57 being tested on the Faustovo firing range. (Russia's MoD)

Left: The Su-57's cannon with 150 rounds is located within the starboard wing root. (UAC)

much earlier. In November 2012, Boris Obnosov announced that the T-50 would start weapon trials 'in the near future'. During the MAKS 2013 airshow, Obnosov complained about the lack of a test aircraft. 'Several types of [internal-carriage] weapons for PAK FA are ready, such as the Kh-58UShK anti-radiation missile', he said at the time, but the aircraft was not yet ready for armament trials.

The Russian MoD released two videos showing the missiles being fired from the Su-57's internal chambers. The first one is the Kh-69 heavy air-to-ground missile launched from the main bay; the second one is the R-74M2 close air combat missile launched from the 'quick launch' bay.

The most important weapons for the Su-57 are new types designed specifically for being carried in internal weapon bays. The Moscow-based Toropov MKB Vympel company makes three new types of air-to-air missiles: close air combat R-74M2 (izdeliye 760) missile, beyond-visual range R-77M (izdeliye 180) and very long-range 'izdeliye 810'; R markings are given by the MoD, while 'izdeliye' (product) are the manufacturer's internal markings. The R-77M and '810' are carried in the large centreline weapon bays and are launched by UVKU-50 catapults, while R-74M2 missiles are carried in side 'quick bays' and launched from VPU-50 rails.

The first of the new AAMs to start firing tests on 8 April 2016, was the R-74M2; it is not known if the shot was fired from an Su-57 or from another aircraft used for experiments. On 26 July 2019, the missile completed the initial tests and was submitted for state evaluations on the Su-57. On 25 March 2020, the Russian MoD released a video in which an Su-57 fighter launching a close air combat AAM from a small weapon bay located at the wing-root section was first introduced; it was supposed to be an R-74M2 missile, although a legacy R-73 or R-74M missile could be provisionally fired with the weapon bay's cover not closed.

The Vympel R-74M2 is a further development of in-service R-74M (AA-11B Archer) with the cross-section reduced so it can be fitted inside the internal 'quick launch' weapons bays of the Su-57. Moreover, the R-74M2 has a new seeker and an improved 516-1M rocket motor that offers increased specific impulse and a longer burn time. Due to its inertial flight control system with radio datalink for mid-course correction (absent on the previous R-73 and R-74 missiles) the weapon can be fired in lock-on-after-launch mode, beginning its flight under inertial control before achieving an in-flight lock-on.

The beyond-visual range Vympel R-77M (izdeliye 180) began flight tests on 28 December 2016. It is an adaptation of the currently produced R-77-1 (izdeliye 170-1; AA-12B Adder) for internal carriage. Externally, the most visible difference is the normal flat tailfins on the R-77M compared with the lattice fins on the R-77. The main reason behind this change is the aim of reducing the missile's aerodynamic drag and radar cross-section. A modernised active radar seeker has increased lock-on range. The new solid-propellant engine features an adjustable pause between the impulses and a larger fuel reserve. Both the path-correction radio datalink and the inertial control system have been improved.

Above: An Su-57 fires an R-74M2 close-air combat missile from the 'quick launch' bay. (Russia's MoD)

Right: A video released by 929 GLITs at Akhtubinsk in September 2020 showed an Su-57 carrying R-77M medium-range air-to-air missiles; this was the first image of this missile ever seen. (Russia's MoD)

During the Army forum in June 2019 in Kubinka, MKB Vympel secured a contract for a production batch (of unknown size) of 'izdeliye 180' missiles for the Su-57. This means that the R-77M will be series-produced at the same Vympel workshops in Moscow as the previous version of the missile, R-77-1.

Finally, on 6 July 2017, firing tests of the very long-range 'izdeliye 810' (its military designation is still unknown) began. The 810 is being developed on the basis of the R-37M (izdeliye 610M; AA-13 Axehead) missile for MiG-31BM interceptor, but has a shape optimised for carriage in the Su-57's internal weapons bay. It also has a new MFBU-810 broadband passive-active radar seeker and an improved engine; the missile's maximum range may be estimated at 186 miles (300km).

Air-to-surface missiles

The most capable long-range air-to-surface weapon designed specifically for the Su-57 is the Kh-69 missile made by the Raduga company from Dubna; it was presented in public only once, in 2015, then with the export designation Kh-59MK2. The missile fully uses the space available in the Su-57 weapon bay; it features a square-section box-shaped airframe with a length of 4.2m (13ft 9in), and a width and height of 40cm (16in); two missiles can be carried in each weapon bay, side-by-side. A deployable 2.45m (8ft) wing is fitted to the top of the box airframe. The launch weight of the missile (all published data refer to the export Kh-59MK2 version) is 770kg (1,698lb).

The Raduga Kh-69 is a counterpart of the MBDA Storm Shadow intended to destroy small, hardened targets of known co-ordinates. For this purpose it has a guidance system borrowed from a strategic cruise missile that includes strap-down inertial navigation corrected by GPS/GLONASS for the cruise phase, and an electro-optical digital scene-matching area correlation system for use close to the target. Powered with a small turbofan, it flies to the target at high subsonic speed. The range declared for export version is 180 miles (290km), limited by the restrictions of the Missile Technology Control Regime; in the version for the Russian Aerospace Forces the range is much longer.

Another heavy weapon dedicated for Su-57 is the Raduga Kh-58UShK anti-radiation missile, a version of the popular Kh-58U (NATO: AS-11 Kilter) with 'cut off' sizes fitted to the Su-57 internal compartment

(K is for Kompaktnaya (compact)) and new wide-band seeker (Sh is for Shirokodiapazonnaya (wide-band)). The missile length is 4.2m (13ft 9in) rather than 4.8m (15ft 9in) in the legacy version; the wing and fins incorporate folding. The declared range for the export Kh-58UShKE version is 152 miles (245km) when launched at supersonic speed and high altitude, or 47 miles (76km) launched at low altitude. An important feature of the Kh-58UShK is its very high Mach 3.6 speed. In 2019, the missile was still in trial.

The KTRV Kh-38M has been in production since about 2016 as the successor of the most popular Russian tactical air-to-ground missiles Kh-25M and Kh-29. The missile flies up to 44 miles (70km), weighs 520kg (1,146lb) and has a length of 4.2m (13ft 9in). The Kh-38M is available in two versions; in addition to the 'internal carriage' missile, there is also a standard version with a larger wing. The guidance variants include semi-active laser, imaging infrared or active radar seekers.

At the end of 2017, flight tests began with the Grom (thunder) missile, which was made by taking the Kh-38M and adding a module with long, folding wings, which was attached under the body, and an extendable empennage. The standard version of the Grom flies up to 75 miles (120km) when launched from a high altitude, or 21 miles (33km) near the ground. The Grom's modification without the engine (but with a larger warhead) covers up to 40 miles (65km). Grom's series production probably began recently.

The smallest air-to-ground missile made specifically for the Su-57 is the 250kg (551lb) KAB-250L electro-optical guided bomb. Boris Obnosov said in February 2020 that the bomb had already completed state evaluations and was ready for production.

On external suspensions the Su-57 can take all types of tactical airborne weapons that exist in Russia.

Long-range Raduga Kh-69 (here under its export designation Kh-59MK2) features a square-section box-shaped body and a folded wing; four such missiles can be carried in Su-57's weapon bays. The range declared for the missile's export version is 290km but the Russian Air Force's version can reach a much longer distance. A Grom winged bomb is seen in the background. (Piotr Butowski)

Internal carriage air-to-ground missiles for the Su-57. All of them have the same length of 4.2m, and their cross-section is in a 40x40cm square, to fit exactly into the Su-57's weapon bay. (Piotr Butowski)

Chapter 9
Future: the Upgraded Su-57M

With the Su-57 (T-50S) fighter entering production and service in the Russian Aerospace Forces, work is underway on its deeply modernised Su-57M (T-50M) version, also known as the 'second stage' Su-57 fighter. Formally, Sukhoi received a contract from the MoD to modernise the fighter on 29 October 2018 although preliminary work began, of course, much earlier. The R&D programme, which is to end up with a ready-for-production modernised version of the fighter, is codenamed 'Megapolis' (megalopolis). It should be remembered that the present Su-57 R&D programme is called 'Stolitsa' (capital city). According to the Russian press, the T-50M prototype is to begin flight tests in mid-2022, and the aircraft is to be ready for production by the end of 2024.

Probably the most important, and certainly the most visible, element of this modernisation is the fitting of new engines. The current AL-41F-1 (izdielije 117) engine powering the Su-57 is a deep modernisation of the fourth-generation AL-31F engine from the Su-27 and Su-30 fighters. During an engine conference on 4 April 2018 in Moscow, the general designer of the Lyulka engine design bureau Yevgeny Marchukov described the AL-41F-1 engine as 'generation 5 minus' and emphasised that it 'has about 80% new components' compared to the AL-31F . It also has much higher thrust and a fully digital control system (FADEC).

The new engine, known so far only from the internal designation 'izdeliye 30', classified in Russia as the 'generation 5 plus', is being developed in the same Lyulka facility in Moscow and will also be produced at the same UMPO plant in Ufa as the current AL-41F-1. The 'izdeliye 30' is a clean-sheet design which is intended to offer increased thrust, lighter weight, a smaller number of elements and lower operating costs. In December 2014, Russia's United Engine Corporation (UEC) head Vladislav Masalov claimed that the 'izdeliye 30' would be '17 to 18 per cent more effective'. If it refers to the full thrust, the new engine should provide 17 tonnes compared to the current 14.5 tonnes. The engine's dry weight may be estimated at 1,450kg (3,197lb), compared to 1,600kg (3,527lb) for the AL-41F-1. Thanks to glass-fibre plastic inlet guide vanes, the new engine fan is to have a much smaller radar cross-section in the front view.

Right: Deputy Defence Minister Yuri Borisov said after the first flight of an Su-57 with an 'izdeliye 30' engine that 'with the new engines the characteristics of Su-57 will improve significantly'. (UAC)

Below: On 5 December 2017, the T-50-2LL with the port engine replaced by a demonstrator of 'izdeliye 30' started the flight tests. (UAC)

The development of 'izdeliye 30' started in 2011 within a research work Demonstrator-PD (PD stands for Perspektivnyi Dvigatyel (future engine)). The engine design was approved by the MoD committee in November 2013; the first experimental hot section of the engine was assembled at the end of 2014, and the first complete demonstrator was run on a ground testbed on 11 November 2016.

Finally, on 5 December 2017, the T-50-2LL (Letayushchaya Laboratoriya (flying testbed)) fighter with the port engine replaced by a demonstrator of the 'izdeliye 30' started the flight tests. Deputy Defence Minister Yuri Borisov said after the first flight that, 'with the new engines the characteristics of Su-57 will improve significantly'.

The expected time for the readiness of the engine, and thus the second-stage fighter, is still being delayed. According to the presentation of the UEC from 2010, the second-stage engine for PAK FA was to enter serial production in 2017. During Aero India in February 2015, the UEC head Vladislav Masalov said that the engine would be ready in 2020. In August 2018, Deputy Defence Minister Aleksey Krivoruchko stated that from 2023, the Russian MoD expected the deliveries of second-stage Su-57 fighters. Not much later, in December 2019, Aleksey Krivoruchko said that the aircraft with new engines was expected to enter service 'in the middle of this decade'.

Meanwhile, a programme to upgrade the AL-41F engine has recently started; the R&D work was codenamed 'Udlinitel' (the extension cord). Perhaps – there is no further information on this subject – it is an alternative in the event of a delay in the programme of the new 'izdielije 30' engine.

In May 2020, Russia's deputy prime minister responsible for the arms industry, Yuri Borisov, said that the modernisation of the Su-57 is much more than just implementation of the new engine. 'Work is being done to expand the combat capabilities of the PAK FA by introduction of advanced long-range weapons.' The equipment of the fighter is constantly being improved. In particular, 'new modes of radar operation are introduced and tested, software is being improved, measures are being introduced to improve reliability and ease of production.'

UAC President Yuri Slyusar declared that Su-57 'will become the basis of the whole family of airplanes, just as earlier the Su-27 became the basis for creation of the family of modern and demanded fighters'. It can be expected that various modifications of the Su-57 will replace Su-33 ship-borne fighters, Su-34 fighter-bombers and MiG-31 interceptors in the distant future.

In an article entitled 'Key aspects of military and technological development of the Russian Federation', written for the directory *National Safety of Russia* in January 2015, the Russian Defence Minister Sergey Shoygu mentioned the PMKI (Perspektivnyi Mnogofunktsyonalnyi Korabelnyi Istrebitel (Future Multirole Ship-borne Fighter)) carrier-based aircraft among future developments. The PMKI would replace the MiG-29K and Su-33 on board new Russian aircraft carriers in the distant future. Most likely, the PMKI will be a carrier-based version of the Su-57 fighter, in the same way that the Su-33 was developed from the Su-27 some 30 years ago.

The Su-57E (T-50-KNS) '057' appeared at the Army 2020 forum in Kubinka with mock-ups of the new 'izdeliye 30' turbofans. (Archive)

A small model of a ship-borne version of the Su-57, supposedly designated Su-57K, as presented together with a model of the new Russian Project 23000 Logovo (den) aircraft carrier. (Piotr Butowski)

Chapter 10

Sukhoi S-70 Okhotnik Unmanned Combat Aircraft

On 14 October 2011, within the framework of the URBK (Udarno-Razvedyvatelnyi Bespilotnyi Kompleks (Strike-Reconnaissance Unmanned Complex)) programme, the Russian MoD ordered Sukhoi to conduct a research project codenamed 'Okhotnik' (hunter). A reported 20 billion roubles (US$600 million based on the then exchange rate) have been assigned to the programme. The Okhotnik programme is to lead to the construction and testing of the demonstrator of a heavy, long-range high-speed strike-reconnaissance unmanned aircraft, S-70.

The Sukhoi S-70B Okhotnik-B demonstrator, number '071', has been constructed at the Novosibirsk Aviation Plant belonging to Sukhoi where it carried out its first taxi trials in November 2018 before being transported on 29 January 2019 by an An-124 to Akhtubinsk, the site of the 929th flight test centre of Russia's MoD, for flight trials. On 3 August 2019, the S-70B took off for the first time performing a 20-minute flight at an altitude of 600m in Akhtubinsk. On 27 September 2019, the Russian MoD published footage of the first flight performed by the S-70B '071' together with the Su-57 '055' fighter. The video presents both aircraft during take-off, common flight and the landing. In the official comment by the MoD, the Su-57 is called 'a leader airplane', while unmanned Okhotnik enables 'extending the radar field of the fighter and target indication for the use by Su-57 of long-range airborne weapons from beyond the air-defence zone'.

Another example of Okhotnik, number '070', was shown to the Minister of Defence Sergey Shoygu and accompanying people in a closed, inaccessible-to-the-public part of the Army 2020 exhibition in September 2020 in Kubinka. It was probably a full-size mock-up intended for on-ground synchronisation of construction components. The Su-57 '057' (T-50-KNS) was standing next to the S-70B.

The Sukhoi S-70 is a large 'flying wing' weighing about 20 tonnes and powered by a single 117BD turbofan, the non-afterburned version of the AL-41F-1 (117) turbofan engine from Su-57. It carries the armament in two internal bays, most likely identical to these of the Su-57 fighter. The armament itself is also common to the Su-57 and S-70. The radar for Okhotnik is made by the same company: Tikhomirov NIIP; it is a simpler version of the Su-57 radar.

In August 2020, Yuri Slyusar, Director General of Russia's UAC said, the MoD has set the task of accelerating the Okhotnik programme 'in order to start deliveries as early as 2024', which is a very ambitious goal. Characterising the Okhotnik, Slyusar emphasised its 'very long combat operational radius and broad nomenclature of weapons'. He also declared that the Okhotnik will be produced in large numbers.

The production version of the Okhotnik was demonstrated in the form of a small model at the UAC hall at MAKS 2019. In the current configuration of the S-70B demonstrator, the eyes are struck by a large, round engine nozzle, definitely not meeting the requirements of reduced visibility. The final S-70 model is smooth; the engine has a flat exhaust nozzle that does not protrude beyond the bounds of the airframe. The shape of the wing tips have changed slightly, becoming rounded.

The T-50-3LL, the third prototype of the Su-57, has been adapted especially for the needs of the Okhotnik programme. It is used for the evaluation of automatic take-off and landing as well as navigation and communication systems developed for the unmanned aircraft. Along with that, the T-50-3LL received a new livery, in the pixelated style of the previous one, but imitating the Okhotnik's shape.

Sukhoi S-70 Okhotnik Specifications (estimated)

Length	14m (46ft)
Wing span	19m (62ft)
Take-off weight	20,000kg
Internal weapon weight	2,800kg (6,173lb)
Maximum speed	1,000km/h
Range	6,000km (3,728 miles)

Above and right: The T-50-3LL is used for the evaluation of automatic take-off and landing as well as navigation and communication systems developed for the Okhotnik unmanned aircraft. Along with that, the aircraft received a new livery imitating the Okhotnik's shape. (Piotr Butowski)

Above: The Sukhoi S-70B '071' unmanned reconnaissance and strike aircraft demonstrator is undergoing tests at Akhtubinsk. (Russia's MoD)

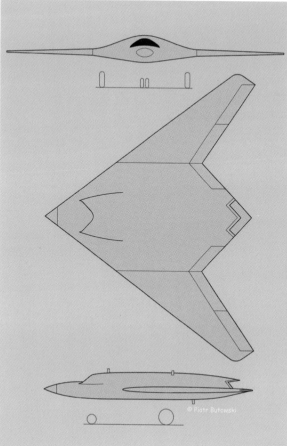

Left: Three views of the Sukhoi S-70 UCAV. (Piotr Butowski)

Below: A model of the production version of the S-70 features a smoothed shape and flat exhaust nozzle. UAC CEO Yuri Slyusar said in 2020 that the MoD has set the task of accelerating the Okhotnik programme 'in order to start deliveries as early as 2024'. (Piotr Butowski)

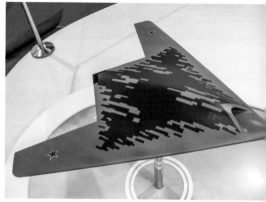

Chapter 11

RSK MiG Does Not Abandon the LMFS Project

The MiG E-721 lightweight fighter, which lost the competition in April 2002 to the Sukhoi T-50 – the future Su-57, is still continued by RSK MiG. However, since there is no order for it, MiG runs the LMFS programme at its own expense at the level of concept research, looking for potential customers.

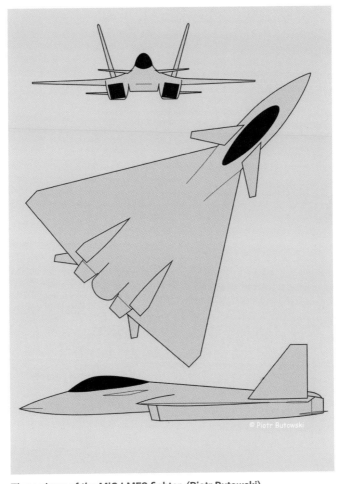

Three views of the MiG LMFS fighter. (Piotr Butowski)

The MiG LMFS is a canard with foreplanes close to the wing, a large triangular wing and small rear control surfaces on the sides of the engine nacelles. This configuration proves that the designers' priority is more manoeuvrability than speed and range, and the main purpose of the LMFS is close air combat. The fighter is similar in size and performance to the MiG-35. The basic set of weapons is carried in one large bay inside the fuselage, most likely the same as the weapons bay of the Su-57 (which has two).

The LMFS is to be powered by two 10–11 tonne UEC-Klimov engines, a further development of the RD-33MK-35 engines from the MiG-35 fighter; in earlier documents they were called VK-10M. The LMFS's equipment and armament will remain in line with the current MiG-35. The Phazotron Zhuk-AME AESA radar for the new fighter will be a modernised version of the Zhuk-AE radar of the MiG-35.

The likelihood of the LMFS being ordered by the Russian MoD is slim. It can be assumed that the LMFS will be offered to India as the basis for India's AMCA project. However, the path to this is not straightforward, as India intends to invite the company that wins the bid for the 114 Multi-Role Fighter Aircraft, announced in April 2018, as a strategic partner in the future AMCA programme. The MiG-35 participates in this contest but has extremely strong competition there. During MAKS 2019, the RSK MiG corporation presented its fighter in the 'renewed export configuration' MiG-35-NG, with a new cockpit, electronic scanning Zhuk-AE radar, as well as a new larger wing and tail.

RSK MiG LMFS Specifications (estimated)

Wingspan	11.5m
Length	15.5m
Maximum take-off weight	24,000–24,500kg
Internal weapons weight	1,500kg
Maximum weapons and stores weight	6,000kg
Maximum speed	Mach 1.8–2.0
Maximum speed at sea level	1,400–1,500km/h
G limit	9
Ceiling	17,000m
Ferry range	4,000km